Aries

21 March – 20 April

First published in Great Britain 2008
by Harlequin Mills & Boon Limited,
Eton House, 18-24 Paradise Road, Richmond, Surrey TW9 1SR

ISBN: 978 0 263 86904 0

Typeset at Midland Typesetters Australia

Harlequin Mills & Boon policy is to use papers that are natural, renewable and recyclable products and made from wood grown in sustainable forests. The logging and manufacturing processes conform to the legal environmental regulations of the country of origin.

Printed and bound in Spain
by Litografia Rosés S.A., Barcelona

About Dadhichi

Dadhichi is one of Australia's foremost astrologers, and is frequently seen on TV and in the media. He has the unique ability to draw from complex astrological theory to provide clear, easily understandable advice and insights for people who want to know what their future may hold.

In the 25 years that Dadhichi has been practising astrology, and conducting face and other esoteric readings, he has provided over 9,000 consultations. His clients include celebrities, political and diplomatic figures and media and corporate identities from all over the world.

Dadhichi's unique blend of astrology and face reading helps people fulfil their true potential. His extensive experience practising western astrology is complemented by his research into the theory and practice of eastern forms of astrology.

Dadhichi has been a guest on many Australian television shows and several of his political and worldwide forecasts have proved uncannily accurate. He has appeared on many of Australia's leading television networks and is a regular columnist for several Australian magazines.

His websites www.astrology.com.au, www.facereader.com and soulmate.com.au which attract hundreds of thousands of visitors each month, offer a wide variety of features, helpful information and services.

Dedicated to The Light of Intuition

Sri V. Krishnaswamy—mentor and friend

With thanks to Julie, Joram, Isaac and Janelle

Welcome from Dadhichi

Dear Friend,

It's a pleasure knowing you're reading this, your astrological forecast for 2009. There's nothing more exciting than looking forward to a bright new year and considering what the stars have in store and how you might make the most of what's on offer in your life.

Apart from the anticipation of what I might predict will happen to you, of what I say about your upcoming luck and good fortune, remember that astrology is first and foremost a tool of personal growth, self-awareness and inner transformation. What 'happens to us' is truly a reflection of what we're giving out; the signals we are transmitting to our world, our universe.

The astrological adage of 'As above, so below' can also be interpreted in a slightly different way when I say 'As within, so without'! In other words, as hard as it is to believe, the world and our experiences of it, or our relationships and circumstances, good or bad, do tend to mirror our own belief systems and mental patterns.

It is for this reason that I thought I'd write a brief introductory note to remind you that the stars are pointers to your wonderful destiny and that you must work with them to realise your highest and most noble goals. The greatest marvel and secret is your own inner self! Astrology reveals these inner secrets of your character, which are the foundation of your life's true purpose.

What is about to happen to you this year is exciting, but what you *do* with this special power of knowledge, how you share your talents with others, and the way you truly enjoy each moment of your life is far more important than knowing *what* will happen. This is the key to a 'superior' kind of happiness. It will start to open up to you when you live in harmony with your true nature as shown by astrology.

I really hope you enjoy your coming twelve months, and gain new insights and fresh perspectives on your life through studying your 2009 horoscope. Here's hoping great success will be yours and health, love and happiness will follow wherever you go.

I leave you now with the words of a wise man, who once said:

Sow a thought, and you reap an act;
Sow an act, and you reap a habit;
Sow a habit, and you reap a character;
Sow a character, and you reap a destiny.
Your thoughts are the architects of your destiny.

Warm regards, and may the stars shine brightly for you in 2009!

Your Astrologer,

Dadhichi Toth

Contents

The Aries Identity

The only way of finding the limits of the possible is by going beyond them into the impossible.

—Arthur C. Clarke

Aries: A Snapshot

Key Characteristics

Determined, fiery, executive skills, born leader, impulsive, headstrong, opinionated, loyal, physical, driven, ambitious

Compatible Star Signs

Leo, Sagittarius and Gemini

Key Life Phrase

I am

Life Goals

To be the best and to be first; to be a leader rather than a follower

Platinum Assets

Enthusiasm, inspiration and fearlessness

Zodiac Totem

The Ram

Zodiac Symbol

♈

Zodiac Facts

First sign of the zodiac; movable, hot and dry

Element

Fire

Famous Arians

Jackie Chan, Elle Macpherson, Ashley Judd, Kate Hudson, Vincent van Gogh, Vince Vaughan, Christopher Walken, Conan O'Brien, David Letterman, Emma Thompson, Ewan McGregor, David Frost, Julian Lennon, Elizabeth Montgomery, Adolf Hitler, Dudley Moore, Sarah Michelle Gellar, Elton John, Timothy Dalton

Key to karma, spirituality and emotional balance

Your past life and karmic imprint is strongly connected to the sign of Sagittarius and Jupiter. In your past incarnation, you were studying and developed your intuitive senses. You now have very strong opinions.

Your key phrase is 'I am'. You have a strong sense of self-awareness, leadership and power, which ensures you a successful life. The Sun is ruling your future karma and promises many accomplishments in life. You attract others who help you achieve your goals.

The Moon rules Mondays and is friendly to your ruler, Mars. Learn to relax more and carry out your meditations on this day. This will accelerate your psychic insights. The new Moon and full Moon are helpful, too.

Your fire element is strong so it's advisable to counter-balance your fast lifestyle. Take calming baths occasionally and use lavender, orange and jasmine oils to relax you and connect with your higher self.

Aries: Your profile

Can anyone ever possibly be too confident, too sure of themselves and their opinions? It seems that some people might think that of the Aries-born individual. But not you! You believe that there can never be enough self-assurance or inner strength to propel you through life, and this is exactly how you choose to live—on your own terms, hard and fast—just like your ruling planet, Mars, the god of war.

To you the journey of life is not for the faint-hearted or for those who wouldn't actively seek what is on offer. Darwin's theory of survival of the fittest is probably the underlying theme of your character, even if you haven't studied the evolution of humankind. You instinctively feel that to get ahead you have to take the first step, and boldly take on the role of the leader.

You understand that the law of the jungle is eat or be eaten, which is why you're mistaken for being a little arrogant and aggressive at times. What do you say about that, Aries? We should set the record straight right here and now. This is mostly a front because behind the fiery mask of your hot and daring character rests a warm and caring spirit.

Friends and lovers who are less superficial than most quickly get to know the real you and, even if from time to time you still annoy them with your 'me-first-I'm-definitely-right' attitude, it's impossible not to love you. This is because you have the knack of making up for any of your imperfections by being truly enthusiastic and inspiring in everything you do.

You are fearless and this excites others. It's occasionally hard to tell whether your courage is bravery or simply rash and impulsive hot-headedness. You love to take on the role of leader and, if you were in a shipwreck or survival situation, it's likely you'd be the first to throw your hat in the ring for the leader's role to help the other survivors to safety.

First and foremost in whatever you do, you crave the element of competitiveness. It's probably true that if the adventure and excitement of the chase wasn't part of the process, the goal wouldn't seem quite as alluring to you. It's the thrill of the journey that attracts you, Aries.

You like to express yourself with absolute honesty and hate any type of pretence. You prefer not to make a friend than play the game of flattery. This is a double-edged sword because most people can't handle your brutal style of honesty. You couldn't care less. They can take you or leave you.

You detest being told what to do so you should preferably work where you are your own boss. You like to be the decision maker and creator of your own destiny. You know that this is a fiery path but feel comfortable with the fact that on your own terms you can become whatever you choose. It would be a mistake for Aries to take a submissive role anywhere. It just isn't in your nature to do so.

Achieving your goals is important to you. You know exactly what you want, and have no problem going after it. Your style is brisk, edgy and uncompromising. People who associate with you soon learn that they have to keep up: if they don't, they'll soon fall by the wayside.

You are impatient when it comes to waiting around for things to happen. There's no dragging your feet on 'Planet Aries' because you kick laziness into the kerb at every opportunity. You tackle life with zeal and enthusiasm and want others to move at your same fast pace. They should be prepared for a hectic and relentless velocity. Give them a seat belt for the cosmic ride with you!

It's quite okay to be pushy from time to time, but don't make it a habit. Come up for air occasionally to see if your crew are swimming in waters out of their depth. Don't automatically assume others can handle the pace you set. This can make it hard for you to be at your best in a team environment, when some people misread your focus as insensitivity or discourtesy. Make an effort to help them keep up with you, and you'll have more friends with whom to share your journey.

Three classes of Aries

If you were born between 21 and 30 March, the planet Mars especially rules you. It dominates your destiny. You can be very severe, both on yourself and others, and don't handle challenges gracefully. You have a tremendous amount of physical vitality and would be well suited to sport and outdoor activities. This is the best form of relaxation for you.

Those of you born between 31 March and 10 April are confident and trustworthy Aries. You have strong links to the fire sign of Leo. You're one of the brightest of the Aries sign and draw others to you very easily. You also love to lead and expect loyalty without question. Your lesson in life is to learn how to use your charm spiritually.

Being born between 11 and 20 April means you are gifted with foresight and other spiritual powers. You are a humanitarian and will be involved with uplifting humanity at some point in your life. Your karma is in the black so many good things will come your way in this lifetime.

Aries role model: David Frost

You can see the Aries individuality in the career style of David Frost, the famous television personality and interviewer. Always direct to the point and keen to extract the most from his guests, he reflects the Aries straight-shooting philosophy. His desire to be number one in his chosen vocation is also a strong Aries trait.

Aries: The light side

People can't help but be drawn to your enthusiasm and bright personality. You stand out in the crowd at a party and for this reason you'll never be short of friends.

You have a way with words and even your personal life seems to be a never-ending sales spiel; you definitely have the gift of the gab. People love it and are enthralled by your quick and interesting stories.

Even though you're impatient and want your way at all costs, you are caring and loyal and will help people wherever you can. Compassion is not your prime character trait, but if you feel someone needs assistance when the chips are down, you will always be there to help them.

You never beat around the bush and are completely honest about your feelings so people will take you or leave you. You have great self-confidence and the courage of your convictions and there's rarely, if ever, any deception about the way you deal with others.

You're not a pretender and your brutal form of honesty is often nerve-wracking to others, but you prefer to deal with the truth, even if others' sensitivities are sometimes affected.

Aries: The shadow side

While you make a fantastic leader in any situation, never allow this to turn into bossiness. It will only make people resent and withdraw their support for you. Leading by example should always be uppermost in your mind and so only act in a way that you'd like others to also act.

You are highly opinionated and, yes, you are right, but not always! You can be quietly assertive without running roughshod over other people's attitudes. Adolf Hitler was the worst case example of an Aries with tyrannical viewpoints.

When ego gets the better of an Aries, it tends to overshadow the most beautiful parts of their character.

You have an immense amount of confidence and your decisiveness is second to none, but when you make a quick decision, you often do it without adequate consultation and this can undermine your personal relationships. Listen to what other people have to say as their contributions may enhance the process of your own success.

Don't be so angry or impatient and don't allow emotional manipulation to interfere with your relationships. By becoming more aware of these shadow traits, you can let the bright sunshine of your personality remove these elements forever.

Aries woman

Your elegant and attractive physique and fiery eyes don't immediately reveal the intensity of your personality until someone digs a little deeper into your character. Everyone knows you're a woman on a mission by the speed of your speech, actions and mannerisms. This is your way of saying: 'Hey, you'd better pay attention to what I have to say, now!' And, of course, you will gain all the interest you want this way.

Elle Macpherson the famous model and fashion designer, is a perfect example of a career-minded Arian girl, with her sleek and attractive physique and larger-than-life ambitions. Aries always wants to be first and women born under this sign are no exception.

You're an extraordinarily creative person and have the ability to spontaneously come up with the goods under pressure. If you want anything done, give it to an Aries woman. People are completely flabbergasted at not only how quickly you can get something done but how professionally as well. You need to slow down, however, as some Aries women tend to live on their nerves.

You have strong opinions and are sometimes seen as too black and white by people. It's not that you don't listen to others' opinions, it's just that you have a sense that you're right and what's annoying to others is that you usually are! You're not the sort of person to get bored easily because you have 101 things on the go at once. It's because of this that the Aries woman is usually successful, can assume responsible positions and is well respected.

Friends feel overpowered by you because your enthusiasm and passion for life is so much more intense than theirs. Try to tone it down for those who haven't yet developed the same level of confidence as you.

Those in your life always know where they stand because of your honesty. Integrity is the keyword for the Aries woman and therefore people don't always like you but they trust your words implicitly. If you say you'll do something, you'll do it on time. And, speaking of getting the job done on time, you must learn to curb your impatience when things aren't happening as quickly as you'd like, or in the way you'd like.

Learn to set yourself realistic timelines so that you can get everything done without stress. Sometimes it seems as if everyone else is moving way too slowly; but actually it's you, Aries: you do tend to move at lightning speeds compared with others.

You'll be successful in life due to your highly ambitious nature and, even if you choose to be a homemaker, tending to your partner and children, this too will not be taken lightly as you want to be the best at whatever you attempt. You are skilful and are considered an ace mother and homemaker.

To offset some of the tension you experience under your star sign, physical exercise is essential not only to help you look and feel good physically, but to calm your mind and emotions and help you direct that effervescent energy of yours.

You lead a hard and fast lifestyle so working out is the best way to decompress.

Your friendships can be rocky, especially if you team up with characters who are just as headstrong as you. You'll need to make compromises as you hate taking a back seat in any relationship.

You love luxury and enjoying the good things in life. Strong colours, especially red, maroon and pink will make you feel great. Being an Aries woman is a statement in itself.

Aries man

It's unlikely you'll overlook an Aries man if he happens to cross your path. He is imposing and sometimes a little louder than the average person. But, a man he is, and there's no disputing that. You see, Aries is ruled by one of the primary masculine planets—Mars. This aggressive, forceful and fiery planet perfectly describes you.

Many famous actors who exhibit these Martian qualities are born under Aries. Take, for example, Jackie Chan and Steven Segal and, would you believe, even one of history's worst despots, Adolf Hitler! Depending on the way an Aries man uses his power, it will determine the constructive or destructive destiny that is in store for him.

In any case, you'll quickly rise to the top of your profession, being confident, skilful and ambitious in your attempts. You have a strong ego and like to showcase that on the world stage. Your swift and fiery energy is pretty hard to compete with and few win in competition against you. Don't to take this to the extreme as there is a possibility that when you are provoked, you could get physical. You have to keep your aggression under control and redirect your energies in positive way, like Jackie Chan or Steven Segal.

Develop patience in your family and social lives. When things aren't going your way, you can get irritable and take out your frustrations on others, much to your later regret. Try to do one thing at a time and at a slower pace. Although you generally get it right, there are times when—even you must admit—your own haste does make waste.

You are sexually powerful and have a strong testosterone level, which is why you'll need a good partner to keep up with your physical drive. They will have to be just as energetic and attractive as yourself to satisfy you. But if you do find someone of this calibre, there are many endearing qualities to make you the perfect partner.

Honesty is one of the male Aries' best traits. Sweeten your opinions and don't try to get in the first or last word. Perhaps you should try a more relaxed attitude to win over the hearts of others?

If you set yourself a task or goal you'll definitely achieve it and will not let anything stand in the way of your objectives. In a working situation others find it hard to work at the same level and drive and with such sustained power as you do. You will need to be more sensitive to the different personalities with whom you deal.

If you are a typical Aries man you need to be surrounded by people who can bolster your sense of self-worth and make you feel needed. You should be careful that this comes from a genuine place within you and is not masking deeper insecurities. Most of the time you don't really need to prove yourself, because Aries is the first and foremost among the zodiac.

Aries child

Are you finding it hard to keep up with the pace of your child? Are they ricocheting bullets off the four walls of your living room, day in and day out? It's quite likely that this describes your high-powered child of Aries! No doubt they're a bundle of warmth and loving energy, but as a parent you'll have your work cut out for you trying to keep up with this breakneck speed.

Arian children need loads of activity to keep them out of mischief. Their ruler, Mars, seems to have them seeking out adventure *and* misadventure. You'll need to keep your eye on them and make sure they don't wander too far, which is something they're prone to do even from a very early age. Prepare them a timetable with many mental and physical activities to keep them occupied and on the right track.

Your Aries child is quite a curious character, who is persistently on the look out for the how, why and where of this world. Impatient in their incessant demands upon you, sooner or later you'll have to ask yourself who's actually running the show: you or them? You'll need to set down strict guidelines early in their lives to make sure they don't get the upper hand. You know, Aries does like to be in charge, and this goes for the youngsters of this star sign as well.

Pushiness and an irritable personality can make them quite a handful to deal with as they're growing up. You'll become exasperated at times as they push you to the limits, but their loving and affectionate nature will more than make up for this. In their teenage years, Aries children can be confrontational if they haven't had enough discipline in their lives. For this reason it's important to get them used to the idea early on.

One of the best ways to rein in your young Aries child is to give them lots of fresh air and sunshine. Teach them the value of good, clean competitive sports, and this will help calm their restlessness and wilfulness.

Make sure that part of your Aries child's schedule allots enough time for sleep and rest as they usually burn the candle at both ends. It's never a dull moment with your Aries child, so it looks set to be a challenging but certainly rewarding experience parenting these zodiac children.

Romance, love and marriage

If you're planning to become involved with an Aries romantically, my first piece of advice is to get ready for an amazing experience. Passion, vivaciousness and an extraordinary level of drive marks their personalities and, if you can't keep up with them, they're going to leave you behind, quick smart!

If you happen to be an Aries and you're reading this you'll know exactly what I'm talking about. Being ruled by active and sexual Mars, you reflect these qualities 100 per cent. Passion is one of your trademarks and pretty well expresses who you are, not just in the bedroom but in your life as a whole. There is no use beating about the bush when saying that sex is of primary importance to you, so any partner of Aries will have to get used to this from the outset of a relationship with you.

Over and above this, your marriage and romantic destiny is strongly governed by Venus and Libra, which happen to govern the seventh zone for Aries. This further accentuates your sensuality, sociable nature and aesthetic attitude, especially in your choice of partners. You need someone who is classy, passionate and loving to fulfil your emotional needs.

Aries love to feel they can showcase the person they love to the world and take great pride in their relationships. You'll attract many partners in your life due to the combined influence of Mars and Venus and will be selective in your choice of 'the one'. You are attracted to and need to prove your prowess, especially if you are a man and born under this sign.

Part of the thrill for you is 'the chase' in love. You love competition as well, so in some ways, the partner who plays hard to get will appeal to you. If someone is competing with you for the hand of that special person you have your eye on, then the stakes are higher and you'll go the extra mile to prove you are better, more passionate and more appealing than anyone on this planet.

Unfortunately, this particular attitude will cause problems for some Aries because the chase turns into an unending series of casual affairs. At the heart of this is your desire to be loved and to prove that you are bigger and better than others. It's important for you to get in touch with yourself and find your own inner security to make your relationships fulfilling and, more importantly, enduring.

If you have a partner who is vital, spontaneous, loving and loyal, you reciprocate their love and affection and want to share the adventure of life and sexual intimacy with them well into your old age. You also like to share your social and professional life with the one you choose. You want someone who will get behind you in your work and serve your eager ambitions.

You work long and hard and may often be conspicuously absent from the home scene in trying to achieve your goals and provide for your family. You need someone who understands your motivation for doing that.

Your love is ardent. Just like Vincent van Gogh who, to prove his love to the one he was enamoured with, cut off his ear as a gift to her. Like him, you're prepared to prove your affection and loyalty to the one to whom you are dedicated.

Another aspect of an Arian in love is your protective instinct. You are imbued with a great amount of courage and never let anything deter you from protecting those you care for. You don't back down when you think you are right and would even lay down your life for your loved ones.

If you choose to have children your Aries character is just as youthful and playful as theirs. You can relate to kids quite easily, being child-like yourself. Your spouses will often wonder whether you're not just another one of the kids in the household because you never seem to grow old. You are playful and have a great sense of humour and love to share fun times with your partner. By developing empathy and passion in your intimate relationships, your Aries character will grow and find even greater fulfilment in the realm of love.

Health, wellbeing and diet

As an Aries you have abundant physical energy. You leave people for dead in the stamina stakes and tend to take on many projects, also working long hours. You must learn that there are limits to what you are able to do, and your restless and impulsive energy could lead to weariness through overwork. This may in turn result in physical stress and strain.

Many workaholics are born under the sign of Aries. Conan O'Brien, David Letterman, Ewan McGregor and Christopher Walken, famous personalities who work long and hard in their chosen professions, are prime examples. Don't overdo it; learn to pay attention to your body's signals.

A positive thing is that you have remarkable recuperative powers and any health problems you encounter are usually short lived. Aries rules the region of the head, which means that headaches, particularly stress headaches, may be something to which you're prone. Sometimes the digestive tract and imbalances in that area are part of the cause. Other problems associated with Aries include dizziness, hearing ailments and nervous dyspepsia.

Because you love to do things quickly, eating is one of your life's activities in which you must definitely slow down. Living such a fast and hectic lifestyle means you probably skip meals and don't chew your food well enough. Chewing your food more thoroughly will help your digestion.

You also like hot and spicy dishes and this can throw out your bodily balance. If you must eat these dishes, take sufficient liquids and cooling foods such as yogurt to counteract their effects on you.

Green, leafy vegetables are great for you, too. You need lots of nutrient-rich vegetables and fruits to give you the added energy you need for your day-to-day activities.

It's better for Aries to eat smaller, more frequent meals because you burn energy at such a high rate. Don't miss meals, even when you are very busy at work. Try to eat only when you're hungry because many Aries tend to overeat, particularly after midlife. If you're upset or angry with someone, it's also not advisable to eat. Reduce your caffeine intake, particularly, as this has a negative effect on your already fast metabolic rate.

Rest when your body tells you it is time to stop and you will surely bypass some of these physical complaints. As a rule your high degree of vitality ensures a healthy life.

Work

Work is a therapeutic activity for you whether you're a corporate animal or a mum at home raising a family; you need to feel productive and useful in society.

You will pursue a profession that gives you variety and change. Anything to do with sports, sales or an entrepreneurial line of work is quite a good choice for you. You're very sociable and like the idea of interacting with groups of people in a working situation.

Careers in which you're able to use your hands can also give you a great deal of satisfaction as you are manually quite dexterous. Some Aries find themselves in military or law enforcement positions because your ruling planet Mars is the god of war. Because of your highly independent character, running your own business at some point in your life will be very appealing.

You are a person of great initiative and inspire those with whom you work. You make a great boss but at times you are a little demanding. Exercise more patience and understanding to those not as experienced or as skilful as you are.

Generally you'll be successful in your work but, if you can curb your impatience, those successes will be all that much sweeter.

Your lucky days

Your luckiest days are Monday, Tuesday, Thursday and Sunday.

Your lucky numbers

Remember that the forecasts given later in the book will help you optimise your chances of winning. Your lucky numbers are:

9, 18, 27, 36, 45, 54

1, 10, 19, 28, 37, 46

3, 12, 21, 30, 48, 57

Your destiny years

Your most important years are 9, 18, 27, 36, 45, 54, 63, 72 and 81.

Star Sign Compatibility

You must look into other people as well as at them.

—Lord Chesterfield

Romantic compatibility

How compatible are you with your current partner, lover or friend? Did you know that astrology can reveal a whole new level of understanding between people simply by looking at their star sign and that of their partner? In this chapter I'd like to share some special insights that will help you better appreciate your strengths and challenges using Sun sign compatibility.

The Sun reflects your drive, willpower and personality. The essential qualities of two star signs blend like two pure colours producing an entirely new colour. Relationships, similarly, produce their own emotional colours when two people interact. The following is a general guide to your romantic prospects with others and how, by knowing the astrological 'colour' of each other, the art of love can help you create a masterpiece.

When reading the following I ask you to remember that no two star signs are ever *totally* incompatible. With effort and compromise, even the most 'difficult' astrological matches can work. Don't close your mind to the full range of life's possibilities! Learning about each other and ourselves is the most important facet of astrology.

Each star sign combination is followed by the elements of those star signs and the result of their combining. For instance, Aries is a fire sign and Aquarius is an air sign, and this combination produces a lot of 'hot air'. Air feeds fire, and fire warms air. In fact, fire requires air. However, not all air and fire combinations work. I have included information about the different birth periods within each star sign and this will throw even more light on your prospects for a fulfilling love life with any star sign you choose.

Good luck in your search for love, and may the stars shine upon you in 2009!

Compatibility quick reference guide

Each of the twelve star signs has a greater or lesser affinity with one another. The quick reference guide on page 30 will show you who's hot and who's not so hot as far as your relationships are concerned.

ARIES + ARIES

Fire + Fire = Explosion

With both of you being ruled by the fiery element and the planet Mars, this is at the very least a warm and endearing match. However, at its very worst it can be quite explosive. It depends on how well you will accommodate each other's egos and which of you is prepared to take the back seat to the other. There is no stepping down from your position and this could be the big difficulty in a match of the two signs being Aries.

I shouldn't commence your compatibility reading sounding so negative because there are some great points of agreement in a combination of the two of you. Firstly, two Aries can be immense fun together and this dynamic duo at any party or social gathering is impossible to overlook. Gregarious and creative, you will always bring vibrant energy to any social situation.

You are very energetic, passionate and exciting, and as a couple you are able to inspire others with your youthful enthusiasm. However, give each other the opportunity in turns to be the centre of attention. It wouldn't be the best idea to be continually playing one-upmanship. Outdoing each other is fine as long as the competition is only in fun.

Quick reference guide: Horoscope compatibility between signs (percentage)

	Aries	Taurus	Gemini	Cancer	Leo	Virgo	Libra	Scorpio	Sagittarius	Capricorn	Aquarius	Pisces
Aries	60	65	65	65	90	45	70	80	90	50	55	65
Taurus	60	70	70	80	70	90	75	85	50	95	80	85
Gemini	70	70	75	60	80	75	90	60	75	50	90	50
Cancer	65	80	60	75	70	75	60	95	55	45	70	90
Leo	90	70	80	70	85	75	65	75	95	45	70	75
Virgo	45	90	75	75	75	70	80	85	70	95	50	70
Libra	70	75	90	60	65	80	80	85	80	85	95	50
Scorpio	80	85	60	95	75	85	85	90	80	65	60	95
Sagittarius	90	50	75	55	95	70	80	85	85	55	60	75
Capricorn	50	95	50	45	45	95	85	65	55	85	70	85
Aquarius	55	80	90	70	70	50	95	60	60	70	80	55
Pisces	65	85	50	90	75	70	50	95	75	85	55	80

It's most important for you to respect each other and give each other enough space to operate independently. If your relationship gets off to a start that is mutually supportive, your combined effort and energy will produce wonderful results individually and as a team.

This is a great connection spiritually as well, because you both have Jupiter ruling your higher ideals. In co-operation you have strong ambitions and will appreciate where each of you is coming from. Taking pleasure in each other's aspirations and occasionally letting go of your own self-absorbed ideas will be a perfect way for you to cement your love.

It's quite likely with the strong physicality of your star sign that you'll want to do many active things together. Sports and other challenging physical hobbies and pastimes will draw you closer. Sexually, the element of fire brings with it much passion and that raw and unbridled love you'll experience at your first meeting will endure over the long term. You'll always maintain a child-like innocence in your relationship and as you grow older you'll still feel as though you are young at heart.

Your best Arian partners are born between 9 and 20 April and these people tend to enhance your good fortune. This is because Jupiter and Sagittarius have a strong influence over them. I see good karma and unexpected material gains from this match.

An argumentative combination is likely if you're drawn to people born between 21 and 30 March. Mars and the double-Aries influence will cause some problems.

Combining your energies with Aries born between 31 March and 10 April is great for your social life and brings with it plenty of physical and sexual attraction. These Arians are to some extent ruled by Leo and the Sun.

ARIES + TAURUS

Fire + Earth = Lava

Taurus is one of the most financially and materially driven signs of the zodiac but for Aries this takes on even greater significance. Right from the outset, you will note that the issues of finance and sharing and whose money is whose will be the key issue for both of you. Finances are best worked out early on if you want to enjoy an enduring partnership.

Taurus is slower and steadier in everything they do and you, Aries, with your impulsive and let's-live-for-the-moment approach to life, will need to compromise and put the brakes on from time to time if you're to make Taurus feel secure with you.

Taurus is imbued with a great deal of commonsense. They are truly steady and strong-willed individuals and some of their down-to-earth advice could help you to a large extent. You could probably end up a wealthier person than you are by joining forces with a Taurus.

You are not accustomed to people challenging you too much but you'll be surprised when the bull of the zodiac, Taurus, takes up your challenge. Although they seem to be laid back, you can expect a Spanish matador versus the bull routine with them. Whatever you do, don't wave the red flag at them, even though this is your primary ruling colour. Taurus is a fixed sign and holds its ground so this could be a head-on collision if you're not careful.

Mars and Venus are the male and female representatives of the zodiac so sexual and romantic activities between you will be sensual, if not raging hot and passionate. There's a loving attraction between an Aries and a Taurus and this will be felt from the start. You will absolutely love the soft and nurturing Taurus, but there is a downside, too. Taurus is sometimes

complacent and this could cause you to look elsewhere for the excitement you need in life.

Taurus is extremely possessive and can be more demanding than you care to be. Your changeable moods might not exactly make Taurus feel as secure and comfortable as they would like, so that's an aspect you will need to work on.

The loyalty Taurus offers you is a positive omen that you could have a good future with them. By co-operation in your lifestyles you will experience considerable happiness together.

Taureans born between 21 and 29 April are probably best suited to you and make great companions. Venus is a very powerful ruler for them and a combination of your energies brings with it loads of passion; possibly even long-term marital stability.

Your intellectual connection with Taureans born between 30 April and 10 May is ideal due to the influence of Mercury. Your discussions will extend into the wee hours of the morning, giving you much continued happiness.

There's a strong spiritual and karmic connection if you team up with someone born between 11 and 21 May. Who knows, this could even be your soulmate if that's what you happen to be looking for.

ARIES + GEMINI

Fire + Air = Hot air

If you need stimulation, and loads of it, you needn't look much further than a Gemini, who will without doubt stimulate your mind *and* your body. The combination of air and fire elements is an excellent one, astrologically speaking. The Gemini quality of air will fan the flames of your passion and make for wonderful social and sexual times together.

Gemini has a great sense of humour, albeit a little dry at times, but you'll enjoy the good times and their witty one-liners. This is the sort of relationship that will bring you out of yourself even more and create a vital relationship. 'Never a dull moment' can best describe this relationship.

Gemini is a little highly strung and so you must take care not to push them too far as their sensitive nervous systems will not keep up with you. You have much more stamina than them, even though their mental powers are surprisingly strong. This is not to say that physically you won't enjoy them or that you can't have a satisfying relationship. It's just that Mars is a far more dynamic planet than their ruler Mercury.

At times a relationship between a Gemini and an Aries will suffer a few setbacks. You need to listen more carefully to a Gemini when they speak. Don't brush over their comments too lightly. They will see your attitude as dismissive and self-centred and this will cause them to become restless. Pay more attention to them and this will draw them to you and result in a more permanent relationship. Your lifestyles are both constantly on the go, so this is another area that needs careful co-ordination for the match to work.

I see this combination working well because Aries will become a great friend to Gemini. Good companionship is always a plus for any relationship, particularly a romantic one, and friendship is a high priority between you as well. Your social lives will constantly be busy.

Sexually, a Gemini will inspire you but you need to stimulate them mentally not just physically for them to feel really deeply satisfied.

Geminis born between 2 and 12 June get along well with you, both romantically and socially. This is a durable partnership because these Geminis have lots of sex appeal and will

easily seduce you. Sex will be an important part of this match and perfectly reflects the best of the fire–air combination.

A relationship with Geminis born between 13 and 21 June is probably better suited to friendship rather than sexual intimacy. Spend time as friends, travelling or generally socially enjoying yourselves together. Dedicate quality time to get to know each other: both of your first impressions may not be quite correct and it would be a shame for you to miss out on a deeper and more enjoyable relationship.

Sometimes disputes are likely with Geminis born between 22 May and 1 June. Unfortunately, you may not get on all that well with them due to their opinionated attitude.

ARIES + CANCER

Fire + Water = Steam

It's quite likely you'll fall head over heels in love with a Cancerian on first meeting them. This is because Mars, your ruling planet, and the Moon, their ruling planet, are astrologically intimate friends. The soft and sensitive lunar vibrations of a Cancer beautifully offset your high-powered personality. The elements of fire and water that respectively belong to Aries and Cancer are quite different but will nevertheless work positively for you, especially in a domestic environment where Cancer functions very well.

Cancer is reserved and at times somewhat shy, but always nurturing and caring. This turns you on in an unusual way and, although it's not quite what you initially look for in relationships, it will nevertheless intrigue you and make you feel more comfortable the more you get to know your Cancerian friend.

Your karma with Cancer will be to connect with their sensitivity and adjust to their unusually volatile moods. As you know, the Moon is constantly changing and just like their

ruling planet Cancerians are chameleons emotionally. You need to learn to go with the flow rather than trying to understand their motivations or trying to control them too much.

Your amazing level of enthusiasm will be an excellent inspiration to Cancer but try not to be too pushy with them. As long as you adapt yourself to their sensitive and intuitive approach to life, you will be able to make considerable headway in your relationship together.

A combination of Aries and Cancer will be excellent as far as family life is concerned, with Mars being the aggressive go-getter who brings home the bacon and Cancer providing a soft place for each family member to land. However, Cancer should be prepared to afford you the freedom and independence that is your primary personality trait.

In sexual affairs you will need to understand that being gung-ho doesn't work. Slow the pace and try a little soft nurturing with them. By remaining aware of the emotional component to this relationship, the two of you will go far.

If born between 22 June and 3 July, these Cancerians may not easily handle your hard-nosed approach to love. These people are thin-skinned characters and you will be constantly treading on eggshells to satisfy them. However, expect plenty of cosy episodes on the home front if you team up with them.

Cancerians born between 4 and 13 July are to some extent ruled by Scorpio and Pluto. This is definitely a powerful love connection between you. Their passionate energy resonates very well with your Aries fire element and you'll immediately feel a strong karmic bond with them.

Those born between 14 and 23 July are not likely to be very satisfying sexually and their idealism will seem all too airy-fairy for you. There is every possibility, however, that a spiritual relationship with them can work wonderfully well because Jupiter is a common karmic planet for both of you.

ARIES + LEO

Fire + Fire = Explosion

This is one of the finest combinations in the zodiac with both of you being ruled by the element of fire. Your attraction to each other is unmistakeable and there's enough dissimilarity in your personalities to keep each other interested. Generally this combination is very satisfying mentally, spiritually and physically as well.

The karmic powers are strong between Aries and Leo and, if you join forces as a couple, I would suggest that material success will naturally flow along with plenty of emotional satisfaction. Being both ambitious and creative, you'll understand each other well and will naturally want to support each other's aspirations, even though at times friendly competitiveness will rear its head. This could be a great professional combination if you choose to travel that path together.

Try to keep in mind that Leo is one of the proudest and most outgoing of the star signs and so your partnership should be based primarily on mutual respect. Both of you like to be seen as number one and therefore you'll need to alternate your egocentric behaviour with the occasional touch of humility.

Fire signs love the world and nature, and love the outdoors. As well, anything that can push their physical bodies to the limit is a distinct turn-on. Because of this I see you both engaging in many fun-filled sporting activities where you can decompress and let off steam that would otherwise create problems in your partnership.

Humour and laughter are also powerful components of this relationship. Leo will make you feel young at heart even if you spend many years growing old together. Why wouldn't you want to give this relationship a good shot?

Because of the common element of fire ruling both your signs, sexually this can be a really hot combination. You'll be satisfied physically and emotionally and you'll both easily fulfil each other's needs. You won't have to guess what turns you on—you'll just intuitively *know*!

Those Leos who seem most suitable to you are born between 13 and 23 August. You'll see much of yourself reflected in them, and they in you. This is a highly stimulating combination, especially sexually. It can be a very playful combination filled with adventure and excitement.

If you connect with Leos born between 24 July and 3 August, you will need to understand that they are the 'Commanders in Chief'. This could present you with a problem due to a battle of wills. This might not be too easy to reconcile in the long term but there will be a lot of mutual respect if nothing else.

Overall fulfilment will be found with a Leo born between 4 and 12 August. This is a good choice for you and your previous lucky karma should come to fruition in your relationship with them. It's lucky for both of you so enjoy it while it lasts.

Generally speaking, Leo is probably one of your best suited signs, even if they are a little too showy for your liking in the first instance.

ARIES + VIRGO

Fire + Earth = Lava

You might find it a little confusing to figure out the cool and modest Virgo. Being so different to your fiery, straightforward Aries personality means that both of you will grapple with each other at the outset. How best to deal with issues of love will be a very interesting exercise for the two of you.

You're passionate, deliberate and often 'in your face'. You don't mince words when it comes to what's on your mind whereas Virgo prefers a more prudent approach and is indeed one of the most sensitive signs of the zodiac.

The elements of fire and earth essentially don't work all that easily because fire is smothered by the earth element. This is not altogether true because a more tolerant approach would reveal to you that Virgo will help direct your power and passion in a most constructive manner. You will gain immense benefits of a practical nature by listening to what Virgo offers you in the way of mundane knowledge.

Unfortunately your patience will run thin as Virgo tries to control each and every detail, the ins and outs of every minor episode of your life as well as theirs! You prefer to steamroll through life using your gut instinct rather than too much meticulous thought power.

Virgo is motivated by service and perfection but you will see this as fussiness and an overly judgemental attitude. Virgos are big-hearted, though, and are able to provide you the help you need to see your ambitions become a reality. Teaming with them could help you in ways you'd never imagined.

If you do choose to work with each other, I assure you that this combination will be very successful, because Virgo will support you completely. You see, Virgo is motivated by two principles: service and perfection. You might describe them as fastidious, but you mustn't be too judgemental.

One big plus is that Virgo is more than happy to listen to all of your ideas and take them seriously. They will then 'tune in' to them and refine them into something that works in practice. On this level, both of you could be quite surprised at how fine a job you do together. And another thing: Virgo is quite happy to take the back seat when all the glory and adulation is being dished out by the world. You'll love being put on the pedestal by them without any ill-feeling on their part.

There's a difference in style, sexually, between you. Virgo is overly hygiene-conscious and needs everything to be ever so perfect before broaching the issue of love and intimacy. You prefer unbridled love that comes from an instinctive urge. This doesn't appear to be the best of matches in the bedroom, does it?

If for some reason you are attracted to a Virgo, those born between 13 and 23 September are most suited to you. You will bring out the best in each other.

I don't recommend a partnership with Virgos born between 3 and 12 September. This is not at all a good combination and will challenge you on every level of your being.

Virgos born between 24 August and 2 September are reasonably well matched, so it's worth considering them before jumping to any negative conclusions.

ARIES + LIBRA

Fire + Air = Hot air

I have personally witnessed some excellent Aries–Libra combinations but by the same token have seen just as many difficult ones as well. I recall one such relationship. A friend of mine who is an Aries with her Libran counterpart spent years in an on–off scenario. What made it even more difficult was that they lived in different countries. They were like the proverbial snake who swallowed a frog that was just a little too big. They could never fully swallow their relationship but neither could they spit it out.

I think this accurately sums up the hit-and-miss nature of a relationship between you: on the one hand, great passion and love due to the Mars–Venus connection, yet the incredibly changeable nature of the partnership due to both Aries and Libra being movable signs.

Another important distinction between Libra and Aries is that Libra isn't as decisive as you. Making a firm decision for them is a long, drawn-out process at times. You, on the other hand, aren't afraid to jump to conclusions, even if it means falling flat on your face. Libra hates to be wrong, but not for the same reason as you. You have a strong ego; they just can't make up their minds!

I believe the two of you should spend sufficient time getting to know each other to understand your differences as well as your similarities. Your signs are opposite each other, and you've heard the saying that opposites attract so you need to understand fully what the different aspects of your personalities really are.

Libra will fan the flames of your passion, but will easily fan the fires of rage and madness just as easily! Libra always has an opinion and you know just how equally opinionated you are as well. Unless you are able to listen without judgement I assure you there will be plenty of disagreements in this relationship.

Social life for both of you is a way you can jointly enjoy each other's company and exercise your need for mobility. In the bedroom, your energies will create a beautiful and exciting union. This is one area I am sure you will both agree on: your compatibility is very well matched. There's an instinctive sexual vibration between the two of you.

You'll easily be attracted to Librans born between 24 September and 3 October, and your initial friendship will quickly develop into a deep love. In this match your ruling planets are quite compatible.

Something special can be expected if you team up with a Libran born between 4 and 13 October. You'll feel responsible for each other, and I should say that if you decide to commit permanently, always keep your dealings with each other above board. Honesty has to be the foundation of this connection.

Librans born between 14 and 23 October find it hard being as practical as you'd like them to be. Mercury is prominent in their lives and, with this excessive activity, could make your practical lives anything but stable.

ARIES + SCORPIO

Fire + Water = Steam

Scorpio has a way of drawing you to them, Aries. There's something arresting about them. You'll love their deep, enticing eyes ... the hypnotic, almost perilous love that is too irresistible to refuse! You're fascinated by the power Scorpio exhibits and in some strange way this is reminiscent of your own power but probably much more subtle. However, let's hope this affair is not like the proverbial moth being drawn to the flame.

This is an intense combination of astrological energies, with Mars being the common factor for both of your star signs. Although you are the element of fire and Scorpio, water, there is a deep affinity between you. You could go so far as to say you are zodiac siblings.

You'll need to be the dominant player in the relationship but will find yourself challenged by Scorpio's subtle and manipulative emotional approach to life and love. Scorpio will often refuse to play by the normal rules, whether in friendship or war. By the time you learn some of their extraordinary tactics you'll learn either to respect them or loathe them, regardless of whether or not you eventually choose to spend your life with them.

This relationship does have the potential to work and in some instances is a powerful force for good. Again, balancing the secretive and subtle energies of Scorpio with your straight-up-and-down, out-front attitude is a nice balance of opposites in many ways. However, you might feel a little threatened and challenged by the reserved vibe of Scorpio, sometimes suspecting things that aren't there. They are indeed a suspicious bunch and this can be unnerving to others. There's no way you'll want to justify your motives for why you do what you do. Scorpio is like the all-seeing eye, and constantly keeps tabs on emotional 'possessions'. You need freedom, not interrogation, of which Scorpio is the master.

Your opinions will clash because your attitudes to life differ considerably. It's best not to discuss certain things and allow Scorpio its deep brooding moments alone. This will turn you on sexually and possibly work to the benefit of the relationship when you decide to kiss and make up after your ferocious disagreements.

Passionate Mars and Pluto dominate you and prod you to love each other deeply. Scorpio will inspire you to look beneath the surface and deepen your view of life and emotional growth will occur in your relationship with them.

With a Scorpio born between 24 October and 4 November, don't expect your conversations always to go smoothly. You will have many disagreements and, as long as you respect each other's opinions, this can still be an asset for both of you in helping you grow intellectually.

Those Scorpios born between 4 and 14 November are idealistically inclined and you'll be fascinated by them, but you need adventure and mobility and that may not be provided to you by this group of Scorpios.

Those born between 15 and 22 November are able to bring some calm to your emotional storm. They are the element of water, with the Moon and Cancer bringing out the softer side of their nature.

ARIES + SAGITTARIUS

Fire + Fire = Explosion

As with the sign of Leo, Sagittarius, the third in the fire triangle of the zodiac, is another no-brainer match for you, Aries. With Sagittarius comes loads of adventure, travel and constant growth. The excitement of being with them really turns you on at every level. This is a relationship of variety, fun and exploration!

There's a sense of innocence and playfulness that you experience when you come together with a Sagittarius and, for some strange reason, probably because the ruling planet of Jupiter for Sagittarius is so benign, you don't feel threatened on an ego level by them.

This doesn't mean Sagittarius is weak or a pushover by any stretch of the imagination; it's just that they don't seem that preoccupied at challenging you every step of the way. In fact, what they bring to the table is quite inspiring mentally and will promote many new lines of thought you'd never entertained before.

I don't suspect boredom will set in with your Sagittarian partner and this is how you like it: continual thrills and a dash of unpredictability, which are all part and parcel of the Aries–Sagittarian combination. You'll have a great tonic effect on Sagittarius and, even if they don't always express their appreciation of you, you'll know they feel supported and inspired by you.

With the fire signs, strong karmic links are sure to bring out the good, the bad and the ugly in your partnership. But that's okay; this is one of those relationships that you instinctively feel is right so a little angst is worth the benefits.

Sagittarius is intuitive, spiritual and concerned with social and global issues. This might be one area that you too will start to take interest in once you join hands with a Sagittarian. Travel and cultural exploration will help broaden your view of the world and your like-mindedness in these areas will result in a co-operative relationship.

Both of you have very strong sexual appetites so your combined fire element will no doubt stimulate your love-making and moments of closeness together. Exploration can be extended into these areas to make life for you continually thrilling in the love department.

Those Sagittarians born between 23 November and 1 December are intimate pals with you and we can go so far as to call them your soulmates. These are the Sagittarians who offer you physical satisfaction as well as mental insights.

If your Sagittarian partner is born between 2 and 11 December you will also sense the extremely powerful connection with them. They reflect back to you many of the qualities you're looking for in a life long partner.

Sagittarians born in the last part of their star sign, that is, between 12 and 22 December, are strong-willed and sometimes even pig-headed. You will find them rigid in their opinions and this will create obstacles if you also border on being a little stubborn yourself. Flexibility will be the key to making this relationship work.

ARIES + CAPRICORN

Fire + Earth = Lava

There are times when a relationship is just so challenging that its success is sometimes a miracle if it works. Unfortunately, the Aries–Capricorn combination is made up of two zodiac signs that are just so diverse that it can be one of the most challenging matches of all. That is not to say it can't be a success, because where there's a will there's a way, but Mars and Saturn, your ruling planets respectively, are such bitter enemies that this is not the type of partnership that finds success easily.

Capricorn, the down to earth, practical, slow and steady sign is rarely known for taking gambles and diving headlong into the adventure of life that you do, Aries. You like spur-of-the-moment action, which probably terrifies your Capricorn counterpart. Your attitudes are just so different that, even if you do find yourself attracted to them, it would take a long while for them to get into the swing of your Aries lifestyle.

Capricorn instinctively feels a need to bring some measure of control to the relationship and will no doubt clip your wings. This will make you feel constrained. If you were to put up with this for some time you would tire of the Capricorn routine, as secure and financially alluring as it might seem. Capricorn is too concerned by financial and material considerations for your taste. Although you aren't averse to this, it's not your primary motivation in life.

Capricorn will feel pushed and uncomfortable with the breakneck speed at which you live life. They need a slower and well-considered routine. Saturn, which rules Capricorn, is extremely uncomfortable in the sign of Aries, whereas your planet attains its greatest power in their sign of Capricorn. This is one of the great astrological anomalies and probably means, as tough as it would be, Aries would fare much better than Capricorn in this relationship.

As with Virgo, the earth sign of Capricorn will steady you and bring plenty of material success if you choose to make a go of it. Making money together would be one of your primary interests once the relationship gets going.

Sexually you are diametrically opposed due to the different qualities of your temperament. Capricorns born between 23 December and 1 January are probably some of the hardest with whom to develop a relationship. Their personalities are inwardly drawn and will therefore not offer you the excitement you're looking for.

Those born between 11 and 20 January are mentally stimulating and so this will be marginally a better match than the previous class just mentioned. These Capricorns will also be a little more compatible sexually.

If you get together with a Capricorn born between 2 and 10 January they too are sexually and emotionally suited to you due to the Venus influence. There is a strong physical attraction between you and these individuals are far better able to express themselves than their other Capricorn brothers and sisters.

ARIES + AQUARIUS

Fire + Air = Hot air

Independence is the keyword for both Aries and Aquarius and, although the astrological elements are different, there is much in common as well. You like the progressive and surprising antics of Aquarius, who is intellectual and also socially orientated. You also like to be part of their social group and feel as if Aquarius gives you enough scope to express yourself and live your life independently.

Aquarians live life on the edge and think in patterns that are ahead of their time. They may even outdo you, Aries! The elements of fire and air are very combustible and bring with them a whole swag of ideas and socially stimulating situations, which is perfect for you.

Both of your egos are very strong but Aquarius is also focused on using their individual power and achievements to uplift society and the world as a whole. Aquarius will silently observe your attitudes and interactions in group situations as well as the larger community. They will judge you on your ability to be as empathetic and compassionate as they are. This could be the make or break of a partnership with them. Aquarians like to be involved with someone they feel is spiritual and progressive. You will need to prove that you are on the path to emotional and spiritual awareness.

You both express yourselves differently when it comes to your independence but somehow I see the differences working out due to your elemental synergy. There will be dynamic responses from both of you towards each other and this will carry over into your sexual affairs as well. There's no doubt there is an attraction between you, and Aquarius is quirky enough to keep your interest between the sheets. You're hot and passionate enough to stimulate them as well. Both of you will be interested in exploring the hidden parts of your psyche and personality and this will result in a sexually fulfilling relationship for you.

For those Aquarians born between 21 and 31 January, you may be a challenge for them by being as headstrong as they are. They are not as adaptable as you and therefore their inflexibility could be a sticking point in this relationship.

Aquarians born in the second part of the sign, from 1 to 9 February, will become close companions being partially ruled by the sign of Gemini. I see a great rapport between you and many good times socially.

If an Aquarian is born between 10 and 19 February they usually have a pretty good sense of humour and will connect with you sexually as well. Venus and Libra strongly rule them so this is an additional factor working to your advantage.

ARIES + PISCES

Fire + Water = Steam

True love will develop between you but there are still some unusual twists and turns in the relationship between Aries and

Pisces that you should be aware of. Think and look before you leap should be the advice to heed before getting too involved with a Pisces. First impressions are lasting and sexually your connection with Pisces is very strong. But Pisces is also very emotional, as shown by the water element ruling them, and your fires may quickly be quelled by this sometimes over-sentimental star sign.

If you stumble upon Pisces and find yourself in some type of socially unaccepted context, such as a clandestine affair or culturally mismatched relationship, there may be an additional dose of excitement that could propel the relationship forward for much longer than it would naturally last. You need to be realistic about your connection together.

Aries, you lead life fearlessly, knocking down the walls of obstruction and elbowing out anything that gets in the way of your ambition. Sensitive Pisces is not so brutal in approach and seems to live life idealistically. This is a tough ideological difference to reconcile between you.

Pisces is not motivated by gain so much as by selfless and spiritual sacrifice. You need to take this into account as your relationship develops. Pisces will open your heart spiritually and give you glimpses of a world beyond this one if you are open to those possibilities.

Pisces will support you on every level unconditionally, even sexually. As long as you're happy to return their love there may be a chance of your partnership working. Just don't take Pisces for granted, because once hurt, they may not be able to rekindle their love for you.

Pisceans born between 20 and 28 February are mismatched with you. The compatibility between you may even cause physical weakness as the electromagnetic energies are at cross-purposes. This is more likely to be a spiritually or socially fulfilling relationship but not ideal as a long-term, committed love relationship.

Pisces born between 1 and 11 March are quite compatible with you and are concerned with their domestic needs and family issues. If you're looking for a cosy and homely life, you may be attracted to these Pisceans.

Passion, love and excitement can be expected with Pisces born between 12 and 20 March. The raging flames of passion and sexual desire are evident with them but you must keep the intensity of your love intact for this to last.

ARIES

2009:
The Year Ahead

Ah, but a man's reach should exceed his grasp, or what's a heaven for?

—Robert Browning

Romance and friendship

Aries, welcome to your new and exciting year! It's a dynamic period for you with your ruling planet Mars and the Sun paving the way for great success in the coming twelve months. You have the magnetic appeal and the determination to go through with your plans and achieve pretty much anything you set your mind to.

Up until the 11th January you will be focused on professional matters but that quickly changes and I see exciting and wonderfully satisfying social opportunities throughout the latter part of January and into February. I also note that you will be surrounded by many new friends as your need to mix with new people will be on the increase.

You won't be satisfied with anything typical and you'll find yourself linking with others who are particularly creative and imaginative. You may even be attracted to someone who has been a long-term friend and this could rekindle your faith in love but might also make you apprehensive.

With Neptune continuing its slow but steady move through the area of friendship, you must remain level-headed and don't let your imagination get the better of you. Be practical, realistic and thorough by looking into the motivations of others. Their expectations and your demands must be balanced on both sides.

Spiritual associations are likely to underpin some of the new relationships that you forge and that will be evident around March when Venus thoroughly lifts your personal prowess to a new level, making you attractive and desirable to friend and stranger alike. You can expect to be showered with affection, gifts and many invitations at this time. Taking part in any group activity will also be very satisfying, both socially and mentally/spiritually.

If you need to make a mark in the world in some way, or feel your self-confidence waning a little, Venus will very quickly put an end to that. Conferences, holidays with friends and also the social activities related to your work will bring you out into the limelight making you even more popular.

You must be careful not to let others tie you up with too many of their problems this year when, especially during the period of April and May, you will find yourself in a confused state of mind, torn between your ideal of being the Good Samaritan, yet on the other hand looking out for your own best interests as well. Use your intuition if you feel someone is trying to take advantage of you. You can't be all things to all people so you must pick your mark, use discrimination, and don't feel bad if you can't help everyone.

April is also important for bringing your long-term partnerships to fruition. It's an excellent period to cement the bonds of love; recommit your love and faith to each other if you happen to already be in a relationship. If you are still on the lookout for your soulmate, April and May are superb months to raise the benchmark of your creative visualisation and send out your best and most positive vibes to the universe to bring you that special person you want to spend your life with.

Passion runs hot in May when Venus and Mars combine and the full Moon in your zone of sexuality offers you numerous love affairs and casual encounters. Seek the advice of trusted friends if you're still confused about the intentions of others, especially during this cycle when your reactions are likely to be quick, fiery and less than well thought out.

Your thinking will be coloured very much by your feelings throughout June, but try not to let negative thoughts cause you any undue stress. Speak your mind but don't project feelings or intentions onto the ones you love. There is a chance you'll misinterpret the words of others and this can impact upon your health. You have a great ability to speak your mind, so do it in a calm and rational manner and this will achieve the desired result.

Work may cause you some problems as you will be unable to devote as much time as you'd like to your loved ones at home. You might find yourself pressurised into doing things simply for the sake of pleasing others. You mustn't sacrifice important projects or deadlines for the sake of keeping the peace. There are times when you can't please all of the people all of the time, and this could be one of them.

A new Moon usually heralds the start of great things and during June the new Moon in your domestic sphere reveals an opportunity to give a facelift to your home, or even make a complete shift to a new residence. Property matters and beautifying your environment will certainly be on your mind.

Throughout July it will be unavoidable—you won't be able to stop yourself from reconnecting with an old flame. With the full Moon triggering changes, a holiday could be on the cards and is just what the doctor ordered. Friendships continue to be strong and a couple of trips or weekends away with a group of friends will help soothe your jaded nerves.

There are strong indications that you may have to confront someone whom you were madly in love with at some earlier time. This can be uncomfortable or you can take it for what it is. Even if you try to avoid the situation you'll be thrown into the lions' den in spite of yourself. Don't let this stress you out too much and, again, the safest way to deal with this is to say as little as possible.

August again brings you romantic opportunities but don't let your sense of inadequacy cause you to miss or overlook vital clues to someone's feelings for you. Mars and Saturn will be creating a high degree of frustration in you, which can be distracting as well as annoying. Be prepared to take some risks around the new Moon of the 20th, as far-fetched and unlikely as the outcome may at first appear. You can develop wonderful friendships this month that can also grow stronger with time.

Serving your friends and helping them with some sort of crisis could be a focus during September. Charitable work and those you care about seem to be very much related. You may also need to wind down some of your outdoor activities, even if the invitations are still coming at you hard and fast. With Mars causing intermittent disruptions from your family or children, you'll need to lay low and deal with these issues, one bushfire at a time.

You mustn't necessarily imagine the advice you receive from others this year will be wise counsel. Question what you hear and don't assume that others know more about something than you. In October, relying on the advice of others without consulting your own inner guidance could be a mistake. If money or goods are the centrepiece of this recommendation, you should heed my warning more seriously. There's a chance you could lose money or simply waste it by not exercising due diligence with those whom you trust too readily.

In late October and throughout the first part of November, communicating and really listening to your partner's grievances will be essential for building a firmer foundation for your future love life. Even if you prefer to keep to yourself and not share some of your plans, which you are still mulling over in your mind, you must make some concessions. Be prepared to listen patiently to the problems of friends and other relatives, even if you don't necessarily have a quick and ready solution at the time. Simply listening to them will be a great help.

Your sexual and physical expression could be thwarted for a few weeks, so the best advice I can give you is to make sure you have plenty of alternative outlets through which to exercise your primal power. Physical activity plus a good dose of creative enterprise should do the trick and help you overcome this temporary obstacle in your personal relationships.

You can gain wonderful new insights into relationships in December and leading up to Christmas will feel as if your communications are back on track. Sentimentality will be strong in the last month of the year with the Moon and Venus influencing your relations.

You might have a strong desire to make contact and have reunions with old school friends and such people you haven't seen for a long while. This could also be a special Christmas as far as your family is concerned. If you have an extended family and they're residing in other places, this could be a year when you actively seek to bring everyone together for a super Christmas reunion.

The year 2009 should be satisfying but I recommend you purchase an extra thick address book to fill it with the names and numbers of the many new people you're likely to encounter in 2009.

Work and money

Your finance planets are Venus, Saturn and Uranus. These planets, particularly Venus, are very powerful as 2009 commences and therefore you have many opportunities that help you forge ahead and increase your income and also your professional standing.

As January kicks off, Mars, the Sun and Pluto jointly occupy your professional sphere. You'll hardly be back at work after your Christmas break and you'll be racing off the blocks to achieve some important objectives in the coming twelve months. It doesn't matter what career you're in, you'll identify strongly with it this year and want to be number one.

Even if you're overloaded by additional responsibilities, you'll gladly take on that role and do extremely well. In the first part of the year there will be no mistaking your drive and competitive spirit. You mustn't allow this high level of energy and ambitions to alienate you from your peers.

In January there's a likelihood you can take on a leadership role as your self-confidence results in a better position or even a new job. My recommendation is that you make your moves early in the year while your vigour is strong.

I assure you that the very lucky placement of fortunate Jupiter in your career sector heralds a new phase in your professional life, particularly as it moves into your profit sector in the first month of the year. It is no understatement that you will see immediate results in your work and finances early in 2009.

This is also an excellent time to expand your circle of working associations and consider connecting with groups, clubs or other organisations that can help you better your professional talents. Friends and co-workers will be very lucky for you and the more time you spend with them learning about their skills, the quicker and more successful you will find yourself in the coming year.

Saturn will continue to meander slowly and steadily through your area of work throughout 2009. It still has some more serious work to complete in your life during this continuing phase. It shows me you'll be demanding so much of yourself that you may undermine your health and vitality. What's the use of being successful, having money and adulation from everyone around you if you're not up to enjoying it physically? Take the time to pamper yourself, pace yourself and carefully balance your material and professional needs with your physical requirements.

This year you will find that working for your own self-centred ideals is not enough. It's a period in which you'll be thinking outside the square and clearly want to help those within and perhaps also those beyond your everyday routine. Humanitarian causes will captivate your attention. Especially from the end of March through until the latter part of April, your work will give you the occasion to help others less privileged than yourself. You'll be called upon to share your expertise and give a hand to others who are not quite as experienced *or* as lucky and well off as you.

In May your passion is strong and apart from any personal implications this indicates a dominant desire to stand out in your working life. This will propel you into June where your desire for financial stability and increased income will have you working longer hours and being much more productive than you've ever been before. You are likely to embroil yourself in monetary differences in your life, however, and you must be careful not to let any of these differences spoil otherwise good relationships.

If you have a say in the way the finances are utilised within your organisation, you will find yourself up against a formidable opponent and must justify your decisions, much to your dissatisfaction. You will take a gamble in August when your ruling planet transits raise the issue of contracts. Your communication will be forceful enough for you to demand what you believe is your right. The new Moon occurs in the fifth zone of speculation in August. This tells me that taking a punt on a workplace agreement or a new job will pay handsome dividends.

With Mars and Saturn entering a challenging phase throughout the latter part of August and September, your frustration with others will reach vexing heights. The full Moon in your twelfth zone of privacy shows that the way to let off steam is to spend some quiet time with yourself away from the crowds and recover your inner composure. You will regain your confidence and sort out some of your professional problems.

With the Sun entering the seventh zone your public relations for the last few months of the year are indeed on an upswing. The full Moon will also be influencing your income in December. This leads me to predict the completion and satisfaction of your financial patterns throughout 2009 with enhanced opportunities into 2010. The secret of your success is to be willing to work hard to create the changes that you desire—but only as long as that work is in keeping with your inner satisfaction.

Karma, luck and meditation

In 2009, the quick shift of Jupiter to your zone of self-fulfilment, life goals and financial increase, is one of the luckiest omens you can expect or hope for, astrologically speaking.

Karma, which relates to the fruits of the efforts you've made, will be fulfilled swiftly in this coming twelve-month period. Believe it or not, your self-composure will also generate great energy, which can be used to boost your luck, wellbeing, popularity and prosperity this year.

People are often taken aback when I tell them how lucky it is that Saturn, the hard taskmaster, has been causing them to work so hard. It is for this reason, and this reason only, that the foundation of your current life cycle is so strong and now allowing you to reap and enjoy the rich harvest of your past efforts. Your hard work is paying off now!

Friends will be instrumental in bringing you luck throughout the coming cycle. You'll have the uncanny knack of being in tune with the prevailing social trends. Somehow you'll be able to adjust accordingly to the requirements of different groups, cultural or socio-ethnic factions and this will make you popular wherever you go. With such popularity it's unlikely you won't attract success, money and love this year.

There are important karmic highlights this year. The full Moon in both March and April takes place in your zone of love and marriage. This two-month period brings emotional satisfaction and plenty of romantic interaction.

The full Moon in July and also in August brings you a second peak of contentment and success. Again, in October there's a hint of marriage for Arians who are single. You can look forward to wonderful new times, social successes, love and material fulfilment during this coming year.

ARIES

2009: Month by Month Predictions

JANUARY

We are what we repeatedly do. Excellence, therefore, is not an act but a habit.

—Aristotle

Highlights of the month

Although your idealism remains extremely high in January, you must be as practical as possible during this first part of 2009. Look to your friends for practical advice, especially those who have their feet firmly planted on the ground. Particularly up until the 10th, you will need to listen carefully to their suggestions. Don't be superficial and miss the finer points of what they have to say.

It's likely that some of your challenging friendships will at last begin to feel the benign influence of Jupiter as it smoothes over any misunderstandings in either work or personal relationships.

Between the 2nd and the 5th you are stimulated by a whole lot of new ideas and your imagination may even start to run a little wild with you. Between the 3rd and the 11th your energy, your drive, is strong in achieving social success. New friendships formed at this time could move to the romantic level quicker than you'd expect. There could also be secret love triangles arising at this time so it's important for you to ask the right questions and establish the status quo of other people's relationships before getting involved with them.

By the 14th, when Venus casts its favourable influence on the Sun, you'll want to take some much-needed time out from work and reward yourself for a job well done. You'll appreciate yourself without any of the past emotional baggage or self-deprecation that has reared its head from time to time. You will also feel inspired by someone older than yourself who is quicker to see your good points than you yourself are.

Your working life is bound to be a source of great pleasure and these older people that I refer to may actually come in the form of professional mentors who are prepared to spend time with you and give you assistance in achieving some of your short-term goals.

You can befriend an important person around the 20th when the Sun moves to your eleventh zone of friendship and more importantly after the 26th with the coming of the new Moon. Don't miss valuable opportunities to put yourself in the right place at the right time. This time requires you also to be watchful of personal friendships that can be sliding into a grey area. Redefining the nature of your involvement with others will be very important this month.

Mercury will highlight the fact that some of your ambitions and plans for success will take on a higher priority. Be focused on those things that matter and discard anything that is distracting you from practically applying yourself. Exercise some of your Arian shrewdness to gain the success you're after in this the first month of 2009.

Romance and friendship

Friendships will start to prosper under these current planetary influences. A new-found friend will turn out to be of service to you on the 2nd, thereby strengthening the bonds of trust and closeness between you. Be mindful of another's jealousy, though.

Flights of fancy characterise the 10th. Your imagination might not be in keeping with the truth of a situation, however. Look at the facts rather than your own spin on a person or situation. Don't let others sway your opinions, especially if your intuition has been a reliable guide lately.

Trying to guide others when you can clearly see a mistake in their behaviour will be fraught with danger on the 13th and 14th. You will have to bite your tongue even if you're asked to act as an advisor. What you have to say will be anything but palatable to them.

On the 20th charitable acts might go unnoticed so don't get all uptight when you run an errand of mercy only to find that you are ignored or dismissed without a thankyou afterwards. An act of kindness should, after all, be done for its own sake, right?

Your emotional and sexual responses will be reciprocated between the 25th and the 28th but may seem to you to be a little overdone! Affection is fine but feeling smothered is a get-me-out-of-here situation. You'll just have to be polite if someone you love is drowning you in unwanted love.

Relationships are a little more normal on the 30th even though you still feel exhausted from some of the heavy duty responsibilities you'll have. Being less vocal and interactive will be your way of bringing yourself to an even greater level of balance and tranquillity over the coming days.

Work and money

Arguments between the1st and the 4th occur if you don't put yourself in the other person's shoes. Listen to what's said. You have to listen with your inner as well as outer ear. There will be vital work clues being given so don't miss what's being said or you just might end up bickering about nothing.

You *think* you want a more superior role. You *think* this will make you happier. Don't make the mistake of believing that there isn't any additional responsibility attached to a coveted position you are chasing on the 13th. Don't be foolish when it comes to assuming power. Look at all sides of the situation, then proceed.

You'll be emotionally charged and making mountains out of molehills between the 18th and the 24th. Don't act on impulses, even if you think you must! Use your rational mind to analyse a work relationship. Someone knows where your hot buttons are and is playing puppeteer with you.

A lull financially doesn't spell disaster at all, so chill out. Redirect your mind to other more positive things than bills and the 'lack of' feeling on the 28th. These are the thoughts that create negative energy around you thus inviting more of the same. You know the drill: 'As a person thinketh, so they become.'

Destiny dates

Positive: 5, 6, 7, 8, 9, 10, 11, 25, 26, 27, 30

Negative: 18, 19, 21, 22, 23, 24

Mixed: 1, 2, 3, 4, 13, 14, 20, 28

FEBRUARY

Highlights of the month

You could well be in two minds this month. Venus accentuates your ego and sense of self around the 3rd and at the same time the new Moon, later in the month, pulls you back into a somewhat dreamy self-absorbed state. Which will it be, Aries? You could try to be both, perhaps.

Do you want to be the centre of attention or would you prefer to stay away from the hustle and bustle of social activity for just a little while? I would suggest you don't waste the beneficial vibrations of Venus during the first two weeks of this month and push forward as hard and fast as you can using the charm and grace that Venus brings with it. You can rest later in the month.

After the 5th, it is clear that you'll have to keep your wits about you in friendship. There will be warring factions and disputes that call for your help in resolving those problems. You'll become very involved in the discussions (heated ones at that) of those you are constantly in touch with on a day-to-day basis. This will be a real challenge for you.

You will find it difficult to bring peace in your camp and it could take as long as the 15th for this to happen when Mercury lends a hand to the situation. Once this cycle is complete you'll breathe a deep sigh of relief.

Between the 18th and the 23rd, when the Sun tugs at your spiritual heartstrings, you will find this five-day period steering you towards a quieter environment and will find it pretty hard to resist. You need some answers but no one on the outside is going to give them to you. This is an inner answer. The flashes of brilliance that come to you will be almost from somewhere unknowable, your higher self or some spiritual guide.

Your values will be challenged this month so it's important to balance tradition with forward thinking, particularly between the 19th and 21st. By the 25th, when the new Moon comes around, you'll be much clearer about what course of action you wish to take. It may be that you're ready to let go of some of the value systems that you've carried and now realise are simply borrowed from others and are no longer of any value to you.

Relationships could be a struggle in the last three or four days of the month as well, and this is also again due to this idea of grappling with authority and conservative values. Trust your instincts and let love—that is, your heart, not your head—help you decide the proper course of action.

Romance and friendship

You are capable of far more courage than you dreamed and can feel it on the 4th. If in the past you were unprepared to try something different romantically, you're likely to do it now and come out with guns blazing.

Finding comfort in your own home will help remove some of your stresses on the 6th and 7th. Entertain in the privacy of your own place and allow your creativity to run wild. On a personal note, don't take your partner's statements to heart on the 9th. They're having a difficult planetary transit.

You need to feel different around the 16th. If only you could change your persona just as you slip in and out of a garment. Who knows, you could try filling your wardrobe with alternative 'me's' and put on a new face every day? Who said you can't? Use the power of Uranus to be different as long as you don't offend anyone.

You're in a bright mood on the 23rd and should continue to be so for the next few days. It's your chance to prove you're as good as you say. With all this sharp and powerful energy there's no reason you can't kick a few goals socially.

Why be mistrustful of your friends on the 25th? It appears that your suspicion has no real cause. This is about your own inner security and self-esteem. Dismiss doubtful thoughts and enjoy the company of friends who are supportive of you.

The Sun now shines a light on your family life and is powerful around the 27th. They say that home is where the heart is and this underlines that fact that your happiness is vitally important in creating the right atmosphere at this time. Give as much as you can now to making life at home beautiful.

Work and money

This is one of the busiest times in the year for you. Mars and Mercury are active planets when in the first few days of the month. You have to let out those frustrations in a way that doesn't offend others on the 2nd and 3rd. For some reason every little thing could go against you. Ah, the planets are doing their thing ... don't sweat the small stuff, though.

You're feeling luxurious and spendthrifty and probably at a time when your head says to cut back on frivolous items. But you won't care on the 10th. It may make you feel good but at some point you'll be staring at the big fat bottom line of a bill. Ouch!

You certainly want to improve your skill sets but also want to party between the 12th and the 22nd. Gaining success requires a sacrifice, though. This is a decision for you and no one else. Balance your social and professional needs.

If you feel devitalised it's because you're working too hard between the 19th and 25th. You need to prioritise your work list and eliminate the unnecessary. Pressure is of your own making and blaming someone else for your lack of time is not warranted.

Destiny dates

Positive: 4, 6, 7, 12, 13, 14, 16, 17, 18, 22, 23, 27

Negative: 2, 3, 5, 9

Mixed: 15, 19, 20, 21, 25

MARCH

Highlights of the month

Working from a base of equilibrium creates a very calming effect on all your affairs in the first two days of the month. By remaining unruffled you can see others' motivations more clearly and will therefore respond with far greater efficiency and impact.

The Moon in your finance zone is strong so you're confident about your own personal abilities and there is a much better likelihood of capitalising on these strengths and converting your energy into cold, hard cash.

Around the 9th some secrets might be revealed and these are not necessarily bad. Gaining a deeper understanding of things is one of the keys to success. By this I mean you shouldn't simply skim the surface of what you're studying, or what you're involved in, as a more thorough investigation will yield gems of wisdom that can also be converted into material benefits.

Secrets do have an impact on your personal affairs, too, however, because at this time you might learn something about a friend or indeed even your lover that could shock you. Maintain that calm tranquil attitude you commenced the month with and you can use this in a positive way rather than letting it bring your relationships undone. Remember: knowledge is power.

On the 15th your mind will be as sharp as ever and this is the time to schedule important meetings, especially if decisions about work and finance have to be made. I wouldn't suggest you even bother about giving things a second thought, as your intuitive powers are strong and your judgement of others is clear and incisive.

When the Sun enters the personal zone of your horoscope around the 21st it brings an immense lift to your physical energies and life circumstances generally. Any competitive actions that must be taken are best done around this time when the Sun enters your birth sign of Aries. Taking on any sort of leadership role or getting into combat and competitive scenarios is excellent and you're likely to come out the victor on all counts.

On the 26th, Mercury brings heightened mental sharpness for you by being in your Sun sign and an idea that you can get the green light. With Venus moving in reverse motion, the contact between these two planets will make your words all the more poetic and convincing. Please don't let your emotions get too involved in the process of negotiation, however.

By the 31st the Mercury and Sun challenge shows you could be a little foggy in your thinking and someone or some circumstance will be misleading to some extent. Don't let nervousness or self-doubt cause you to say or do the wrong thing. This is still a winning cycle for you, Aries.

Romance and friendship

There's a subtle joy in kicking everyone to the kerb when you need a little 'me time'. It could be one of those days on the 3rd. You don't have to make excuses or give reasons to a friend when you tell them that you want to be alone. It's a great way to make up some extra time. They'll understand.

You're dreaming of love and romance but don't have the guts to act upon those dreams. If you have someone in your line of fire, what's the point if you don't shoot? You need courage and determination, even if you think you don't have a chance of snaring a good catch. On the full Moon of the 11th the worst case scenario is a 'no'. So, go for it!

You're busy and active and in no mood for anyone to get in your road. Put up that sign that says do not disturb if you want your space clear of others. Family members need to understand that if they aren't as energetic in their chores you'll be reading them the riot act. Yep, you're on a mission at this time.

You have to be a little sneaky if you're to get away to some secret rendezvous without upsetting work commitments on the 16th. You know you shouldn't because others will bear the brunt of the extra work you land them with. So, what to do? Work harder, smarter and postpone the event. Everyone will end up happy.

A sudden infatuation with a new person on the block is short lived around the 21st, so don't spend too much time daydreaming on what might be. Get real and focus on what is! Don't mistake egocentric behaviour for self-confidence, either. Perceived value is often different to a subjective view of ourselves. Your personal efforts might miss the mark on the 27th and you'll kick yourself for a lost romantic opportunity. Better to understate your case on the 28th.

Work and money

You have unexpected outgoings and must make allowances on the 9th. Taxes and other annoying term payments will chew up time in research around the 13th. If you can bypass the detail, well and good; otherwise you'll miss a social engagement.

A miscommunication is the last thing you need, especially if it relates to your employment or, God forbid, a new job or interview. Take time to be extra careful listening to directions and appointment times on the 19th. Don't blow it because you have a successful opportunity.

Are you developing a penchant for nocturnalism? Are you wandering the corridors late at night in the wee hours, trying to get some shut eye? You'll be a super creative insomniac between the 23rd and the 26th and need extra hours to get everything done. You either have to get rid of some activities or get used to that sleepy feeling.

Your reaction time is quick and your words sharp on the 30th. You can win the battle for sure but the war will continue and you may not win it in the end. Smooth talk, sweetness and other subtle manoeuvres are superior in winning over others.

Destiny dates

Positive: 3, 9, 15, 23, 24, 25, 26

Negative: 9, 19, 31

Mixed: 16, 21, 30

APRIL

Highlights of the month

You're no April's fool, particularly this year, Aries, and with Mercury bringing you the added bonus of a very practical bent of mind you'll be financially on top of things this month.

Nobody will be able to pull the wool over your eyes and between the 1st and 10th make sure you leave no stone unturned, ask as many questions as you feel are necessary to give you satisfaction, and be the wheeler and dealer if you want to be.

All of this culminates around the full Moon of the 9th, with any business transaction or perhaps emotional negotiations bringing a sense of relief at that time. It is, however, quite likely that this will have a stronger bearing on your financial affairs as Mercury moves into gear in your finance zone around the 10th.

Venus is oscillating between your zone of self-confidence and zone of hidden secrets. On the 11th you might need a little time out from your relationships as you reassess whether or not they are indeed your soulmate. You could simply be bored. It's up to you to be the hero in the relationship if you want it to work. Shine your brightest light, be the best you can, and set the standard for the future of any partnership you happen to be in.

On the 20th the Sun influences your family life and this, along with the new Moon of the 25th, has a bearing on the way you use your finances for the upliftment of your relatives and loved ones. You will find yourself discussing the ways and means your clan can pool their resources so each of you can gain some additional financial leverage.

Sometime around the 22nd, however, when Mars enters your Sun sign, you will want to work on your own independent path with the result that others could see you as selfish and insensitive. Perhaps after assessing your own needs you should think carefully on how to balance them against the needs of the group for the best results.

All through this period up till the 25th your head will be lost among financial paperwork, banking and other monetary odds and ends. This will give you much satisfaction and, even if you haven't previously been that involved in business affairs, you could develop a taste for it at this time.

Along with this, Mars brings with it a certain level of impatience and pushiness. Try to not be too forceful in your opinions as it could alienate others and bring the reverse result of what you desire. At least you'll be prepared to independently strike out on your own and develop some new methods in your professional life, too.

Romance and friendship

There are some people you'll never outdo and that can be annoying. This is particularly hard if you love them and are in a deep relationship. True love means accepting another human being—warts and all. That means accepting unconditionally. So, stop brooding on it or get out. A decision along these lines has to be made on the 8th.

Don't think about the past on the 13th because it will ensnare you in 'would have, could have, should have' thoughts, which are fruitless. You can't change what was. You can only live this moment in a way that will yield better results in the future. Don't be drawn into arguments over past mistakes.

Don't take no for an answer as persistence pays off on the 16th. You have to look at just how much time and energy you've invested in someone to realise that this isn't necessarily a lost cause yet. Back off for a moment and regroup your energies. Then pounce again!

Disputes with friends are short-lived on the 21st because it's really a storm in a teacup. Don't let minor differences in your attitudes explode into unreal proportions. Listen to others' opinions and hold back from speaking your mind till you've heard the whole story.

You can feel charming, attractive and maybe even ten years younger on the 25th, with Venus supporting your personal energy. Rely on these positive traits to win the day. There's no doubt that someone carrying Cupid's arrow is lurking in the shadows, so be on the lookout!

Work and money

Your clever wit and your ideas are ten steps ahead of other slow coaches on the 4th. If people don't understand where you're coming from they aren't going to accept what's on offer. Simple/stupid is the approach if you're busting to close a deal or business negotiation.

Sudden travels and meetings can throw you into a tailspin on the 6th if other aspects of your routine aren't up to date. Get organised so that you can enjoy some material benefits as well as mental peace. You're double-booked and may not know it.

Refocus your mind on money matters on the 10th. Don't let your emotions dictate the plan, however, as you may be impulsive and spend more than you are able to afford. Keeping up with the Jones's will be an issue, so tighten your belt.

Work can be less bothersome as you near the completion of a project on the 18th. Don't be so quick to jump on the next bandwagon as you can well afford to take a breather. You don't have to play the superhero—you've already proved yourself. Play the relaxed and successful character who deserves an extended lunch break between the 20th and 25th.

A job offer you've held high hopes for could turn out to be a dud on the 27th. If you place too much expectation on this you'll end up being disappointed. Try to be realistic in your judgement.

Destiny dates

Positive: 1, 2, 3, 4, 5, 7, 9, 10, 16, 18, 20, 22, 23, 24, 25

Negative: 11, 13, 27

Mixed: 6, 8, 21

MAY

Highlights of the month

Learning, education, communication and anything that can expand your mind is the name of the game during the month of May. It's most definitely a month of exploring and expanding your mental horizons.

Mercury, which is the fastest moving planet, races into your zone of communication bringing with it a whirlwind of activity and possibly the danger of stoking the fire with far too many irons. I must point out that it is important that you focus as much as you can on your line of expertise rather than branching out into too many areas, as exciting and alluring as that may be.

It could be a flare up emotionally with the presence of Mars in your Sun sign and this will continue throughout the month of May. Your spouse or partner may not be amenable to the far-reaching plans and ambitious ideas that you exhibit. You would have to coax them, my friend, and lead them gently through those uncharted waters.

As I said earlier, you must educate yourself and it's an excellent time for you to enrol in new courses, to travel to different environments to enlarge your base of knowledge by gathering as much information as you can. You'll meet all sorts of people. You'll even be quite surprised at how neighbours, brothers and sisters and other work colleagues will turn out to be a valuable source of information. They will inspire you to live outside your normal humdrum routine and you'll start to get a taste for a whole new round of experiences on the mental plane.

There are some important turning points for you this month and they are the 7th, 14th and also the 16th. On these dates, try to listen more than you speak as an incorrect judgement on your part will be caused by nothing other than too much of your own self-absorption or inflated ego. Remain humble and don't assume you know more than others during these important planetary transits.

Your mentally active cycle continues and is enhanced when the Sun enters your zone of communications around the 21st. Meeting with others who are on a journey and communicating with people at a distance will be prevalent around this time of the month and, on the new Moon of the 24th, an important discussion is spotlighted, bringing with it some important breakthroughs.

On the 28th love affairs are high on your list of priorities. To make these work, try not to dredge up the past and keep rehashing stories or topics that you know can't be resolved and over which neither you nor your partner have any power. Maintain the peace to finish off the month of May in a good frame of mind.

Romance and friendship

Stay away from others for a while if you need to collect your thoughts and get some additional perspective on things. The chatter of people will annoy you and create a reactive tendency between the 3rd and 5th. You'll uncover a truth on the 8th that will hold you in good stead.

Communication with a friend feels as if they are strangers once again on the 15th. You know there's something brewing beneath the surface but can't quite put your finger on it. It could be a hot flame—beware—you might get that finger burnt!

If you're hanging your hat on the decisions of others, don't hold your breath. Indecision is the order of the day and you're best to make your own plans irrespective of others' promises on the 20th. You could end up waiting around all day without a clue about what's actually happening.

Brilliant thoughts need to be tempered with decisive action on the 24th and 25th. Others won't understand the implication of your ideas or your motives. Being too progressive will alienate others, even your allies. Try to feed them your concepts gradually.

Romance is better than usual on the 28th and you have the charisma to back any new meeting with a potentially fun future relationship. Choices will be hard, especially if two or even three potential lovers arrive simultaneously.

Too much of a good thing can lead to later health issues. Curb your diet, watch your health, sleep more and stress less are the key pointers to a better health on the 30th. A romance is likely to be sizzling hot; but, do you have what it takes to sustain it?

Work and money

Emotional responses will lose you Brownie points on the work front on the 2nd and 3rd. Stick to the issues in any professional debate and don't get hot under the collar. A workmate is under duress and you'll have to rescue them; even if they resist your measures to get them out of the, er, 'mud'.

Expect some positive news in your work on the 12th. Your efforts will pay off even if you thought you'd missed the boat.

Improving your service skills will further enhance your opportunities in the coming months as well as impressing the right people.

Between the 18th and 20th, sleepless nights aren't the result of any particular worry, just an inability to turn off the mental chatter. This requires discipline on your part and perhaps a little meditation or deep breathing will calm your mind. Don't eat late at night. That might have something to do with the problem.

Overwork must be balanced with some fun and entertainment. Why are you punishing yourself? Is it for the money? Are you trying to prove just how much resolve you have? Believe it or not, a relaxed and fun attitude can help accelerate your success. Try enjoying yourself a little more at the end of the month, especially on the 28th and 29th.

Destiny dates

Positive: 8, 12, 21, 28, 29

Negative: 2, 3, 7, 14, 15, 16, 18, 19, 20

Mixed: 24, 25, 30

JUNE

Highlights of the month

That you wish to fulfil your desires as quickly as possible is shown by the close proximity of Venus and Mars, and also Mars moves into your financial sector on the 1st.

Instant gratification will spill over into many areas of your life and include such things as food; drink, sex and even excessive work practices where your motivation is to get across the finishing line first. This will be triggered by the Moon and Saturn in your work sphere.

You will be feeling less than satisfied with some of your efforts; but remember, working harder is not necessarily working smarter and this impulsive streak I foresee will have the effect of causing you to make errors of judgement thereby requiring a re-do of the work at hand. Proceed more slowly and cautiously, thereby avoiding the double-handling situation.

The new Moon is in your domestic zone this month, along with the full Moon in your zone of higher ideals and philosophy. This is interesting insomuch as it highlights important developments in your family life and a recommitment to the values of caring, nurturing and devotion. This is a great time to re-establish the importance of your family ties and perhaps delve into your family roots in some way. You will discover some things about your past family ties. Putting down your roots is also a possible reflection of these planetary influences.

Because the full Moon of the 7th has relevance to long journeys, there is also a strong hint at a reconnection with family members from afar. Try to keep in touch with brothers and sisters and those who have made a life in different places within your country, or even overseas, as this will be a source of great satisfaction to all of you.

In the last part of June for Aries, you may decide to make a quick change with your mode of transport. Even if you perhaps have a car, you may choose to purchase a new one and spend lavishly in so doing. Any form of travel will also be attractive to you as the Sun causes you to be very restless. Is that an itch I detect in your feet?

Watch your finances on the 26th and 27th as your debts will run a little higher than you expect. Try to make an effort to keep your filing cabinets and diaries in a better state between the 28th and 30th. For many people, tax and filling out all that paperwork can be a little confusing and exhausting as well. You should come through this unscathed but the word to watch out for this month is 'impulse'. Think before you leap!

Romance and friendship

Be careful of disagreements with friends on the 3rd. You react to opinions that normally don't bother you. If something else is troubling you, don't project this onto the wrong person. It may take you considerably longer to make amends if you burn them.

Thinking of the past can make you ill if you're focusing on the bad stuff rather than the good. You must look at the tough times as a sort of positive material for improving your future. Change your perspective and look at the upside on the 7th.

The dust is settling after a rather unusual emotional interaction with a loved one on the 12th. This will leave you confused as to whether or not the friendship is worth it all. But don't make hasty decisions just yet—wait for a few days before the final word.

The travel bug will start to bite around the 20th. Are you prepared? Do you have visas, passports, brochures, tickets and other paraphernalia to make it a success? Don't cut corners and, incidentally, you need to speak to your employers about the time off.

A sweet note or email can help pick up the pace on the 24th and give you a renewed sense of confidence in yourself, especially if you're single. Don't be afraid to play the game, even if romance seems a little complicated now. Someone is very intriguing and just as attractive on the 28th.

You'll be busy around the home and want a major change. A cosmetic facelift for your house or apartment is just what you need to pick up your spirits around the 29th. If you're going to do this, be prepared to spend money to make it look a million bucks.

Work and money

You're more emotional than usual and need someone as a sounding board to bounce off your feelings. There are vague sensations about your career, which are puzzling on the 9th. Should you move forward and try harder, or walk away? Make a list of the pros and cons before you think any further ahead.

A little soul searching can help reorient your mind at a time when the hustle and bustle of the world is crowding you. Others may not understand your logic on the 12th; but who cares! Spend a little time alone to work out some of your career issues.

Avoid gambling between the 13th and the 24th, even if you're invited to a swanky casino or club. Mars's impulsive vibes will cause you to act rashly and to overlook the appropriate time to walk away with a win, as small as it may be. Love affairs are risky, too.

You have an opportunity to travel in an eastern direction for work on the 21st. Travel with a friend and this will be a thoroughly enjoyable day in which you both gain new professional knowledge and win over the hearts of clients as well.

Destiny dates

Positive: 1, 7, 28, 29, 30

Negative: 3, 9, 13, 14, 15, 16, 17, 18, 19, 22, 23, 26, 27

Mixed: 12, 20, 21, 24

JULY

Highlights of the month

The full Moon in your career sector creates a tug of war between your domestic duties and professional responsibilities this month. You'll have to be clever in the way you divide your loyalties. You'll try hard to please someone only to find that someone else has a complaint about your attitude and the fact that you've ignored them. You can't win sometimes, no matter how hard you try to please others.

By the 2nd your important relationships will come into focus. The people who butter your bread (pay you your salary) and other respectful figures will now feature strongly in your life. Deal with these people and you will hone your skills to make the right impression on them.

Between the 4th and 7th, you'll have some slight relief from work when Mercury enters your zone of domestic bliss. Take time to sort out issues that demand your attention before beginning a new line of work on the 8th. A challenging opportunity is attractive to you and you mustn't have any fears that your skills will have shortcomings. Venus will help you in your interviews and a deal should be secured easily during this second week of the month.

It's best to force your hand in some contractual negotiation before the 9th, before Mercury moves to a hard aspect with the Sun. Something will go against your best interests, or the terms you'd agreed to will suddenly change. The world is awash with Indian givers and it would be a shame to lose momentum through someone turning the tables on you.

Something in your neighbourhood will bother you after the 12th. If it's the council digging up your road at 1 am, neighbourhood squabbles or catfights, you'll find it hard to sleep. Expect some rattled nerves and general tiredness from lack of sleep. You'll have to grin and bear it until the 18th when Mars enters your lucky fifth house.

You will either find yourself on the winning end of a gamble at the racetrack or club between the 19th and 21st. Staring into the eyes of a brand-new lover is sometimes a gamble, too, isn't it, Aries? This cycle brings with it a lot of creative flair and flirting is certainly not out of the question when we ponder how your creativity might now best be explored.

There's a strong focus on your children between the 22nd and 28th. Take the time to listen to their issues, give them a soft place to land and understand that, even if they're young, they are fully aware of what is going on and may even take you to task for something you've done.

The month finishes with a good judgement coming your way.

Romance and friendship

Let your family members know they are responsible for what happens to them as they made the decisions in the first place. Someone will be trying to enforce their brand of victim-hood on you on the 5th.

Bring some peace to your peer group between the 9th and the 11th. Speak to your friends about deeper issues that can truly make a difference to them. If you assume they are not interested in what you have to say philosophically, they could be missing out on the benefits of your wisdom.

Between the 10th and the 16th you might begin a new love relationship and it can start so suddenly and progress so quickly that it could turn your head. Rely on the trusted advice of a friend if you feel things are moving too quickly.

You can't expect everything to be black and white so it will be important for you to take time out and study the various shades of grey between the 18th and 21st. You'll want to do this so that you can adequately do away with any people that are holding you back.

Stand your ground and fight for your beliefs on the 24th. If you weaken and withdraw you'll make life harder for yourself with little hope of recovering your position. A show of strength is what's needed.

Your mind will be racing through a million and one things from the 25th to the 27th. Slow down and tackle each task one by one. Prioritise your jobs and refuse social distractions. You'll come out a winner and be free of concerns as a result.

Your attraction quotient is high on the 28th and 29th, with the possibility of winning a few new hearts in the process. Love is certainly in the air as Venus and Mars bring new friendships your way.

Work and money

You can push for what you believe is yours in love but might alienate colleagues in the process on the 7th. Satisfying your boss and your own ambitions means walking a fine line. Be fair but firm at the same time. Your strength will win you respect.

Trust what you feel on the 9th and don't believe a tall story that sounds way too far-fetched. If you're on the lookout for a new job there's no need to throw out your principles for it. You want integrity, too, don't you?

Friends will rally to your cause if you're not too proud to ask for help on the 18th. Playing the game of martyrdom isn't going to help you finish your work on time or fulfil your deadlines. Ask for help if and when you need it, especially by the 20th.

A call related to work is good news and can create some excitement on the 25th—and just when you thought life was getting a little dreary! Be ready with some witty one-liners and a new outfit to use on the occasion if an appointment is secured.

Destiny dates

Positive: 2, 4, 5, 6, 8, 9, 10, 11, 22, 23, 28

Negative: 5

Mixed: 7, 12, 13, 14, 15, 16, 17, 18, 19, 20, 21, 24, 25, 26, 27

AUGUST

Highlights of the month

Some Aries will have had strained relations with their mothers or older female members of their family over the previous months (possibly even years). With the entry of Venus into the zone relating to your mother, it will be an almost magical effect which lifts the fog and reunites you in body, mind and soul with them.

You'll be making greater efforts to hear their side of the story rather than shutting down and turning your back on what's being said. I foresee a fondness and better appreciation for your mother's view and she will take on much greater importance in your life at this time.

If you've had a desire to beautify your home, the period of the 16th to the 21st is the time to make the necessary arrangements to do so. Venus will bring with it an increased sense of colour, balance and harmony. Your previously wayward view of furnishing and interior design is now somehow improved and your knack for creating an elegant home interior is bolstered, making you an amateur interior designer, at least temporarily. You can have a lot of fun choosing colours, fabrics and even furniture that will give your whole domestic sphere and lifestyle a completely new facelift.

The Sun enters into a wonderful phase now with sports and other types of competitive physical activity stimulating you to get outdoors and get your red Arian blood pumping hard once again. It will not only rekindle your vitality but will also reconnect you with people you've lost contact with. The new Moon on the 20th reflects a brand new cycle of sporting interests in you and this will mean a greater level of energy and attractiveness being revealed to the world around you.

And, speaking of relationships, Mercury swinging around into your seventh zone of marriage will start the ball rolling on a whole new approach to the way you conduct your relationships. If you're seriously committed to your partner, talking about long-term stability, domestic responsibility and possibly even marriage will take place after the 22nd. You are ready to settle down and will want to test the same level of commitment in your partner.

By the 27th you'll see that your sincerity in talking about how you feel will have a tonic effect on your partner, causing them to open their hearts to you. Greater transparency and a deepening of the bonds of love are what I see for you in the last few days of August.

Romance and friendship

Being a homebody for a few days will be comforting *and* stimulating on the 7th—believe it or not. You need your own space for two or three days and this gives you the opportunity to catch up on an old favourite hobby or simply just do nothing.

A deep and meaningful conversation on the 14th yields better results than expected and sets the trend for a new phase in a relationship or close friendship. Don't be afraid to speak you mind. Your honesty will tear down the walls of separation!

You're on top of your game and a few new opportunities greet you on the 18th. Give more time to leisure as you need a relaxed mind to cope with mounting pressures. Your inner resolve is strong and successes at work are assured in the coming weeks.

You are attractive after the 22nd and not because of anything physical so much as your changing attitude. Your energy is strong and so don't be surprised to draw unusual and interesting people into your field of activity over the coming days.

Over-emotionalism with family members is distracting on the 29th. Are you able to retire to a quiet corner for a while, away from meddling nuisances of others? And take the phone off the hook for a while, I suggest!

Your affections are powerful around the 30th and 31st and love should find you even if you can't find IT! More mature and steady partners are preferred now as you want to put your roots down and settle down. For attached Arians, this is a time of more committed love.

Work and money

You might feel annoyed over elements in your professional life on the 3rd but realise there's not much that can be done other than grinning and bearing it. Help is hard to find and responsibilities will seem heavier than usual. The tension will pass.

Your energy and willpower is strong and your desires will be fulfilled without too much drama on the 9th. Job prospects you consider are successful on the 12th with a promise of higher income!

Money issues postponed on the 20th will create problems down the track. Do today's tasks immediately or you'll forget the numbers and terms of engagement. Don't sweep your financial worries under the rug or they'll come back to haunt you sooner than you think.

On the 24th, biding your time will seem like a waste of time as impatience gets the better of you. Dashing to the finishing line will seem more important, but you know you are only robbing yourself of the precious moment called NOW. Slow down and smell the roses for a while. You'll eventually get there—wherever 'there' happens to be.

Destiny dates

Positive: 7, 12, 14, 16, 17, 18, 19, 21, 22, 27, 30, 31

Negative: 3, 9, 24, 29

Mixed: 20

SEPTEMBER

Highlights of the month

A demanding work schedule is very likely throughout September, so please, Aries, take the time to sit down in the first few days of the month and plan your diary, reassess your appointments, and make sure that you're not double-booked or perhaps overwhelming yourself with too much work.

You do have the opportunity on the 3rd and 4th to slow the pace, take the phone off the hook and carefully monitor where your month is going. If you can do this (as much as your impulsive nature will struggle against it), you'll be able to set down a far more realistic calendar for September.

On the 6th you'll feel more confident and able to draw strength and resources from the people that work with you. You have to figure out who's with you and who's against you on the 7th. The Moon will be causing some friction and especially with someone that is usually your bedrock and reliable support.

Mercury re-enters your zone of work around the 18th and you have to separate the chaff from the wheat, the allies from the enemies, and the important from the insignificant during this mini-phase of the month. Hard work is necessary up until the new Moon of the 19th, when the quick change in your daily office routine will bring greater productivity for you.

Around the 22nd, coming head to head with someone you normally work with may also be necessary as there's no point allowing ill-feelings to build up to unmanageable proportions. Mars will be moving slowly into a better relationship with Saturn in this phase. Although you think that all hell could break loose by broaching an irritating subject, you'll be totally amazed when you receive a cordial response and agreement from a work colleague. Don't have any fear about speaking your mind, as honesty and integrity will be seen as your motivation.

During this same period of the 16th to 21st, you have to work hard at balancing your exercise and dietary needs with a heavy workload. You mustn't skimp meals, sleep too little or party too hard as this will adversely affect your performance in the coming weeks.

Things will improve all-round on the 23rd when the Sun enters your zone of involvement with others. You will feel so much more relaxed with others and partnerships will be slowly taking on greater importance.

On the 30th Venus makes a lovely aspect to the Sun and brings you an opportunity for partying, joyfulness and a sharing of good feelings.

Romance and friendship

Reconnecting with past friends and others from yesteryear will be an important aspect of your karmic cycle between the 3rd and the 13th. Communicating with long-forgotten friends is not a bad idea on the 12th. Don't be too forceful, though; they may have changed their style just as you have.

Your mouth might be ahead of your mind, which is ahead of your actions, on the 18th. This is all in reverse sequence, you realise! Think carefully before speaking your mind. Even if you reveal the whole truth and nothing but the truth it's going to be misunderstood. Silence is superior.

Up to the 21st the illusion of 'what could be' will be preferable to your current romance, or so it seems. Irrational and unrealistic advances in the pursuit of an illusion will be like a thirsty person in the desert finally arriving at a mirage lake and drinking a glass of sand. Be careful of what you desire—it isn't what it seems.

Your spiritual search is strong and so interest in philosophical and ethical issues are high on your agenda between the 23rd and 25th. Bringing lofty concepts down to the human level requires your touch of genius. Living an ideal is far harder than reading about it.

You're much happier at home on the 28th, or should be now that a lot of the dust around a relationship has settled. The times may not be so exciting or passionate but at least indecision and unsettledness are resolved. It's time to relax for a while.

Your mind is indecisive about an offer of love around the 30th. You will not be in possession of all the facts and need them before committing yourself. A friend you haven't contacted for a while might be part of the solution. Give them a call and ask their opinion.

Work and money

It's easy to get stuck in a particular way of doing things, especially if you're not feeling up to par on the 4th. Your business and professional routine is at the heart of this and you could be due for a major overhaul. Don't be scared of change. It will increase your vitality.

An expected raise may be delayed or not on the horizon as expected on the 9th. If you've built plans around extra money this could be frustrating; but what can you do? Cutting back is the only other option until your boss or Providence decides otherwise.

You need to jump away from any impending debts, which you see as obvious traps on the 16th. Playing daredevil with your money will cause a head-on collision with your credit card statements. This is all a matter of suppressing your desire for shopping therapy.

On the 29th your astute communications skills will currently require you to intervene between two opposing parties to help determine the outcome of a certain event. Make sure you discern the proper approach as you should neither help nor hinder either party but should simply offer your impartial advice to both.

Destiny dates

Positive: 3, 4, 5, 6, 8, 10, 11, 12, 13, 23, 24, 25, 28

Negative: 4, 22

Mixed: 7, 9, 12, 16, 17, 18, 19, 20, 21, 29, 30

OCTOBER

Highlights of the month

Outdated relationships are sure to end this month, so be prepared to take some important steps. Expect a big shake-up on all fronts, Aries.

On the 4th you'll be at cross-purposes with the desires of others in your environment. Your opinions will clash and, if you're not careful, you could assume that a powerful disagreement is an indicator that every aspect of your life with the one you love is doomed to failure. Don't go magnifying these problems out of proportion because you must work on the similarities rather than the differences if you are to have a successful relationship.

If you're not yet planning your work well enough, your sleep patterns will continue to be adversely affected with disturbing dreams and uncomfortable energies causing you less than restful sleep, particularly between the 10th and 12th.

You must recommit to your resolutions to improve yourself in all areas of your life. Sign up for that gym membership or jazzercise class around the 14th, and continue to make this a habit. It will not only help you sleep better but will knock the edge off some of your competitive and irritable states of mind. You'll see an immediate softening of your communication style, which will in turn bring back the buzz into your closest one-on-one relationships.

October is a month in which long-term relationships start to prosper. The work of the previous couple of months is starting to pay off emotionally. This is stronger when Venus enters your zone of marriage on the 15th. Again there is a new mini-cycle that can show marked developments in the way you express yourself in relationships and the way others show their love to you.

Simultaneously, Mars affects your love affairs and shows that you will be competing for the attention of someone in your social group. A lover will become an object of your obsessive attention but they will have their eye on someone else. You must be careful to define clearly the limits to which you will go to gain their affection. If you take the limits too far, you will undermine your own self-respect.

From the 18th the Sun prods you to inspect the deeper mysteries of your life and inner self. This commences a stage of self-transformation that has little to do with any of the outer trappings of life. Meditation, psychology and philosophy become intriguing to you to such an extent that you will join some study groups or philosophical organisation that can help accelerate your self-awareness.

Quick journeys after the 20th help you gain greater perspective on your current state of affairs. Getting away from everything for a while has some intangible benefits as well. The last week of the month shows a keen desire to work hard and put in a few extra hours on the job. Again, you may well have revitalised yourself but don't drain yourself all over again. Conservation will be your keyword just now.

Romance and friendship

If you've been hiding or lacking in confidence, get out and about on the 4th. Moving beyond your home turf will expand your mind and give you a taste of different cultures and views. Love affairs or romantic interludes with a slightly different cultural leaning are also likely up to the 12th.

Love and money are tied together on the 16th. Finances might get in the road of smooth emotional dealings. Greater interest in your partner will impact favourably on the outcome of negotiations, so give more weight to matters of the heart than cold facts and figures.

Unsavoury elements in your relationship will be out of your control by the 22nd. What you *can* control is your reaction to your partner, but not theirs to you! You must overlook the nuisance value of a problem in favour of keeping things in a state of equilibrium. Home matters should take precedence on the 24th, so don't let anything intrude on your personal space.

An effervescent attitude will attract more than one interested potential lover on the 26th. You have a lively and bubbly energy that will create excitement in those with whom you come into contact. There's a chance you will win someone's heart by the 29th. There are romantic overtones associated with this current planetary cycle.

An Aquarian or Libran could start to become part of your daily affairs on the 30th. New friendships are likely to arise while travelling. Initiate action to make yourself more popular.

Work and money

You may feel that you are oscillating between two extreme courses of action on the 7th—one of retreat and the other of daring audacity. If you're swayed by the opinions of others you will ultimately regret not relying on your own instincts and taking the less safe path. Although the advice of others will appear secure, remember that empires can be built on a gamble.

Don't only look at the short-term savings on a purchase on the 14th because in the long run it will cost more than you plan for. Don't allow a tight-fisted attitude to get the better of your good commercial sense. Look closely at the service aspect of any equipment you consider.

There are ways and means of reprimanding others if you happen to be calling the shots in your work. Diplomacy is a skill and doesn't require anger or crass behaviour on your part to get your message across. You'll be dealing with someone's poor behaviour on the 23rd and 24th, but this will only be effective if you can maintain your own self-control.

Your industriousness and dependability will show through on the 25th and whatever you have attempted can be completed with full confidence. If the going has been tough don't give up now or you'll throw out all that good work for nothing!

Destiny dates

Positive: 14, 15, 16, 18, 20, 25, 26, 29, 30

Negative: 10, 11, 12, 22, 23

Mixed: 4, 7, 14, 24

NOVEMBER

Highlights of the month

Such things as sex, money and shared resources are all important during the month of November. You can have access to or should I say, excess of, these things, especially leading up to the 8th when Venus nudges you and your sensuality towards emotionally stormy but exciting times.

The new Moon of the 16th tells it all and you will be prepared to try something very different in the area of your intimate relationships. Don't be too radical in how you propose this to your partner, however, as it might scare them off. Make sure that you wrap your proposals in lots of loving affection, as this will bring you the response you seek.

The full Moon is important this month as is the new Moon of the 16th showing you that between the 2nd and 16th your personal awareness will achieve important emotional breakthroughs. This will not be something easily discerned or explained other than to say you feel changes taking place within yourself. During these types of cycles I thoroughly suggest you play spectator to the grand sport of life and not judge yourself or others too readily. Simply observing what takes place can be a great teacher in itself.

These very attitudes will have a marked influence on your professional activities between the 19th and 23rd, when your poise and self-containment will be noted by people who are in a position to open doors for you. You'll be a great example to others who may not be able to quite pinpoint what is changing within you, but that change will be obvious and will help you in this closing chapter of the year.

Your karma is becoming ripe now and this will be evident around the 25th when the Moon indicates that you will make contact with powerful elements of your past. Some event will happen at this time that exposes hidden memories, mysteries or things long forgotten. These recollections will help piece together the jigsaw of your life. How often have you heard it said, or have said yourself: 'What's life all about?' This time the favourable influence of the planets will give you a peek into the true answers to these questions. This month will go a long way in helping to sort out some of your longstanding issues in relationships.

This month is also very, very significant in that Saturn, the chief planet of karma, enters your relationship sphere. Some of the changes I am referring to in your own experience may be happening equally or perhaps even more strongly in the lives of a very important lover or partner. You need to remain aware of these things over the coming months and deal with others with a greater degree of sensitivity.

Romance and friendship

A special opportunity to enjoy passion, romance and the possibility of a long-term relationship is likely during the full Moon of the 2nd. Because your zest for life is so high, a desirable person will be drawn closer to you and will also stimulate your interests.

Revive your relationship on the 13th, especially if you've been lazy in demonstrating your love. You might be finding it easier to do your Sodoku or word puzzles at night when your partner wants greater intimacy. Make an effort because what you put in is what you get out of a relationship.

Forcing someone to love is wrong, wrong, WRONG! Subtlety and finesse is the way on the 18th. Say less, remain elusive and let your charm woo them. Playing the power broker will only alienate the very person you're trying to attract. And don't try to involve third parties to do your dirty work: that will backfire, too!

You have to trust your instincts when it comes to love on the 24th and the 25th. You have the right energy to make a strong impact socially but won't feel as confident as you should. Compliments might not be trusted as you feel people have ulterior motives. Believe in yourself first and everything will fall into place.

On the 27th a friendship might leave a bad taste in your mouth but will re-surface later for a shot at revival. How will you deal with that? You need to lay the ground rules before getting involved so you don't have to subject yourself to complicated decision making later.

There's no point biting your tongue if you need to make your opinions known on the 30th. You'll be exploding at the seams if you've held back from telling someone just how they should act. Take them aside and reveal your true feelings to them. It will clear the air and make you feel 100 per cent better.

Work and money

Your mind will naturally gravitate towards financial matters on the 3rd and you can achieve much that was previously swept under the rug. Planning effectively will give you peace of mind and add a few extra dollars to your bank account.

A friend has some great news that can financially benefit you on the 5th. Make time to take in the moment, get away from social distractions and do what you can to gain some monetary benefits as a result. On the other hand, their reliability and butterfly behaviour might frustrate you and trigger distrust.

You can make changes between the 10th and 19th but you must act quickly. Time is of the essence if you want to revamp your professional circumstances. Write your resignation letter, because procrastination will kill the moment and leave you stranded on the desert island of dissatisfaction.

Reclaim what is rightfully yours on the 22nd—not just materially but emotionally. If things have skewed in a workplace relationship you can reorient the connection to a better state of affairs. If your interaction has soured it's up to you to make the effort to prove yourself again, otherwise get out and stop wasting valuable time.

Destiny dates

Positive: 2, 3, 4, 5, 6, 7, 8, 9, 10, 11, 12, 13, 14, 15, 16, 17, 19, 20, 21, 22, 23, 24, 25

Negative: 27, 30

Mixed: 8, 18, 22, 25

DECEMBER

Highlights of the month

You will be walking the fence between giving attention to the material affairs of your life as opposed to the intellectual and spiritual side. This does appear to be a common theme throughout the last few months, doesn't it, Aries?

With the Moon coming to fullness on the 2nd, my prediction is that you will give greater weight to your intellectual and spiritual self, especially with Mercury, Sun and Venus impacting your realm of higher knowledge. This will reach a peak on the 16th around the new Moon when 2009 comes to a stage of completion for most Aries.

You mustn't question too much but rather just accept the strong flow of energies towards and through you. Use this in the best way possible by making peace at home, listening carefully to what your spouse or partner has to say and also by completing any unfinished business.

Between the 9th and 14th give special consideration to someone who needs you to be there; if not to solve a problem, but simply to listen with open ears and an equally open heart.

Between the 16th and 19th you'll have a last minute rush-job finishing up all those niggling little odds and ends prior to

Christmas. Finish as much as you can but don't get distracted on the 20th when friends try to tempt you with an alluring social engagement that will only make work harder for you a day or two later.

When the Sun enters the tenth house of your career on the 22nd, some end-of-year achievement based upon your organisational ability will make you very much talked about. This is a great conclusion to the year and takes you into Christmas feeling satisfied that the work you've done throughout the previous twelve months has really been worth it.

Around the same time, between the 21st and 23rd, a friend will pressurise you into taking on some of their problems and this is wholly and solely due to their own lack of self-management and discipline. You will be well aware of this but could buckle under the pressure of being a Good Samaritan. If you can clearly see you are being used, I suggest that it would be a grave error for you to give in and take an extra load on your shoulders just at a time when others more deserving will utilise the gifts of your time and love more appreciatively.

In these last few days of the month and year of 2009, my best advice is to not be a sucker for a hard luck story, hold your head high and enjoy the rich rewards that the year has brought to you.

Romance and friendship

A fortuitous meeting means the start of great things on the 5th. An introduction to someone with a whole new slant on life can be inspiring intellectually but also very practical at the same time. Be receptive to any new friendships.

There's no point arguing about love on the 13th, especially if you know that the problem is due to your own pigheadedness. Humility is the keyword where discussions about your love life start spiralling into World War Three. There are a few important lessons to be learned. Listen carefully to achieve a deeper understanding.

If you take up a friend's unexpected offer to travel somewhere on the 16th you'll be richly rewarded on many levels. Getting yourself out of your day-to-day rut at this time is essential. Your heart is yearning for some new experiences and travelling is one of the ways to get them.

Martyrdom is the predominant theme of your life between the 20th and the 23rd, and there won't be any shortage of victims wanting your services (and stupidity, either!). Why are you feeding fuel to the fire when you know someone is capable of dealing with their own problems? Stop giving away your time and energy!

Confusion regarding a friend is inevitable on the 26th. Neptune causes you to worry about something you or they have said. Look at people for who they are and don't judge them. An admirer will be a wily character. Be on guard.

Your drive to achieve a better position at work will be fulfilled but you must be prepared to sacrifice a friend or two on the way. The stars are hinting at envy in the shadows. You'll sense this but mustn't play into the spider's trap. Rest on your own laurels and self-confidence on the 29th.

Work and money

You're in your own element on the 6th and your words will carry great weight wherever you go. A business or creative idea is brilliant and you need to trust your instincts. If you're pitching a concept, don't take no for an answer on the 8th.

You can't always deal with things personally. In fact, a face to face confrontation can sometimes backfire. Between the 10th and the 12th you'll need to get someone else to do your dirty work, especially if the problem has to do with people who are just not listening to you. Enlist the help of someone stronger and more neutral.

A problem that you are currently dealing with is the seed of something quite positive. You are not looking at the issue from the correct perspective. On the 19th you can turn a financial debt into a moneymaking opportunity if you look at the problem with a fresh set of eyes.

A windfall or coveted position is yours on the 26th and paves the way for some exciting and successful transitions in your life. Get ready to do some serious celebrating. Just don't spend too much of the money before it lands in your bank account, though.

Destiny dates

Positive: 2, 5, 6, 8, 29

Negative: 21, 23

Mixed: 9, 10, 11, 12, 13, 14, 16, 17, 18, 19, 20, 22, 26

ARIES

2009: Astronumerology

Every man has in himself a continent of undiscovered character. Happy is he who acts as the Columbus to his own soul

—Sir J. Stephen

The power behind your name

By adding the numbers of your name you can see which planet is ruling you. Each of the letters of the alphabet is assigned a number, which is tabled below. These numbers are ruled by the planets. This is according to the ancient Chaldean system of numerology and is very different to the Pythagorean system to which many refer.

Each number is assigned a planet:

AIQJY	**=**	**1**	**Sun**
BKR	**=**	**2**	**Moon**
CGLS	**=**	**3**	**Jupiter**
DMT	**=**	**4**	**Uranus**
EHNX	**=**	**5**	**Mercury**
UVW	**=**	**6**	**Venus**
OZ	**=**	**7**	**Neptune**
FP	**=**	**8**	**Saturn**
—	**=**	**9**	**Mars**

Notice that the number 9 is not allotted a letter because it is considered special. Once the numbers have been added you will see that a single planet rules your name and personal affairs. Many famous actors, writers and musicians change their names to attract the energy of a luckier planet. You can experiment with the table and try new names or add letters of your second name to see how that vibration suits you. It's a lot of fun!

Here is an example of how to find out the power of your name. If your name is John Smith, calculate the ruling planet by correlating each letter to a number in the table like this:

J O H N   S M I T H

1 7 5 5   3 4 1 4 5

Now add the numbers like this:

1 + 7 + 5 + 5 + 3 + 4 + 1 + 4 + 5 = 35

Then add 3 + 5 = 8

The ruling number of John Smith's name is 8, which is ruled by Saturn. Now study the name-number table to reveal the power of your name. The numbers 3 and 5 will also play a secondary role in John's character and destiny so in this case you would also study the effects of Jupiter and Mercury.

Name-number table

Your name number	Ruling planet	Your name characteristics
1	Sun	Charismatic personality. Great vitality and life force. Physically active and outgoing. Attracts good friends and individuals in powerful positions. Good government connections. Intelligent, dramatic, showy and successful. A loyal number for relationships.
2	Moon	Soft, emotional temperament. Changeable moods but psychic, intuitive senses. Imaginative nature and compassionate expression of feelings. Loves family, mother and home life. Night owl who probably needs more sleep.

		Success with the public and/or the opposite sex.
3	Jupiter	Outgoing, optimistic number with lucky overtones. Attracts opportunities without trying. Good sense of timing. Religious or spiritual aspirations. Can investigate the meaning of life. Loves to travel and explore the world and people.
4	Uranus	Explosive personality with many quirky aspects. Likes the untried and untested. Forward thinking, with many unusual friends. Gets bored easily so needs plenty of stimulating experiences. Innovative, technological and creative. Wilful and stubborn when wants to be. Unexpected events in life may be positive or negative.
5	Mercury	Quick-thinking mind with great powers of speech. Extremely active life; always on the go and lives on nervous energy. Youthful attitude and never grows old. Looks younger than actual age. Young friends and humorous disposition. Loves reading and writing.
6	Venus	Charming personality. Graceful and attractive character, who cherishes friends and social life. Musical or artistic interests. Good for money making as well as numerous love affairs. Career in

		the public eye is possible. Loves family but is often overly concerned by friends.
7	Neptune	Intuitive, spiritual and self-sacrificing nature. Easily duped by those who need help. Loves to dream of life's possibilities. Has healing powers. Dreams are revealing and prophetic. Loves the water and will have many journeys in life. Spiritual aspirations dominate worldly desires.
8	Saturn	Hard-working, focused individual with slow but certain success. Incredible concentration and self-sacrifice for a goal. Money orientated but generous when trust is gained. Professional but may be a hard taskmaster. Demands highest standards and needs to learn to enjoy life a little more.
9	Mars	Incredible physical drive and ambition. Sports and outdoor activities are keys to health. Combative and likes to work and play just as hard. Protective of family, friends and territory. Individual tastes in life but is also self-absorbed. Needs to listen to others' advice to gain greater success.

Your 2009 planetary ruler

Astrology and numerology are closely linked. Each planet rules over a number between 1 and 9. Both your name and your birth date are ruled by planetary energies. Here are the planets and their ruling numbers:

1 Sun; 2 Moon; 3 Jupiter; 4 Uranus; 5 Mercury; 6 Venus; 7 Neptune; 8 Saturn; 9 Mars

Simply add the numbers of your birth date and the year in question to find out which planet will control the coming year for you. Here is an example:

If you were born on 12 November, add the numerals 1 and 2 (12, your day of birth) and 1 and 1 (11, your month of birth) to the year in question, in this case 2009 (current year), like this:

Add 1 + 2 + 1 + 1 + 2 + 0 + 0 + 9 = 16

Then add these numbers again: 1 + 6 = 7

The planet ruling your individual karma for 2009 will be Neptune because this planet rules the number 7.

You can even take your ruling name number as shown on page 113 and add it to the year in question to throw more light on your coming personal affairs like this:

John Smith = 8

Year coming = 2009

Add 8 + 2 + 0 + 0 + 9 = 19

Add 1 + 9 = 10

Add 1 + 0 = 1

This is the ruling year number using your name number as a basis. Therefore, study the Sun's (number 1) influence for 2009. Enjoy!

1 = Year of the Sun

Overview

The Sun is the brightest object in the heavens and rules number 1 and the sign of Leo. Because of this the coming year will bring you great success and popularity.

You'll be full of life and radiant vibrations and are more than ready to tackle your new nine-year cycle, which begins now. Any new projects you commence are likely to be successful.

Your health and vitality will be very strong and your stamina at its peak. Even if you happen to have the odd problem with your health, your recuperative power will be strong.

You have tremendous magnetism this year so social popularity won't be a problem for you. I see many new friends and lovers coming into your life. Expect loads of invitations to parties and fun-filled outings. Just don't take your health for granted as you're likely to burn the candle at both ends.

With success coming your way, don't let it go to your head. You must maintain humility, which will make you even more popular in the coming year.

Love and pleasure

This is an important cycle for renewing your love and connections with your family, particularly if you have children. The Sun is connected with the sign of Leo and therefore brings an increase in musical and theatrical activities. Entertainment and other creative hobbies will be high on your agenda and bring you a great sense of satisfaction.

Work

You won't have to make too much effort to be successful this year as the brightness of the Sun will draw opportunities to you. Changes in work are likely and if you have been concerned that opportunities are few and far between, 2009 will be different. You can expect some sort of promotion or an increase in income because your employers will take special note of your skills and service orientation.

Improving your luck

Leo is the ruler of number 1 and therefore, if you're born under this star sign, 2009 will be particularly lucky. For others, July and August, the months of Leo, will bring good fortune. The 1st, 8th, 15th and 22nd hours of Sundays especially will give you a unique sort of luck in any sort of competition or activities generally. Keep your eye out for those born under Leo as they may be able to contribute something to your life and may even have a karmic connection to you. This is a particularly important year for your destiny.

Your lucky numbers in this coming cycle are 1, 10, 19 and 28.

2 = Year of the Moon

Overview

There's nothing more soothing than the cool light of the full Moon on a clear night. The Moon is emotional and receptive and controls your destiny in 2009. If you're able to use the positive energies of the Moon, it will be a great year in which you can realign and improve your relationships, particularly with family members.

Making a commitment to becoming a better person and bringing your emotions under control will also dominate your thinking. Try not to let your emotions get the better of you throughout the coming year because you may be drawn into the changeable nature of these lunar vibrations as well. If you fail to keep control of your emotional life you'll later regret some of your actions. You must carefully blend thinking with feeling to arrive at the best results. Your luck throughout 2009 will certainly be determined by the state of your mind.

Because the Moon and the sign of Cancer rule the number 2 there is a certain amount of change to be expected this year. Keep your feelings steady and don't let your heart rule your head.

Love and pleasure

Your primary concern in 2009 will be your home and family life. You'll be keen to finally take on those renovations, or work on your garden. You may even think of buying a new home. You can at last carry out some of those plans and make your dreams come true. If you find yourself a little more temperamental than usual, do some extra meditation and spend time alone until you sort this out. You mustn't withhold your feelings from your partner as this will only create frustration.

Work

During 2009 your focus will be primarily on feelings and family; however, this doesn't mean you can't make great strides in your work as well. The Moon rules the general public and what you might find is that special opportunities and connections with the world at large present themselves to you. You could be working with large numbers of people.

If you're looking for a better work opportunity, try to focus your attention on women who can give you a hand. Use your intuition as it will be finely tuned this year. Work and career success depends upon your instincts.

Improving your luck

The sign of Cancer is your ruler this year and because the Moon rules Mondays, both this day of the week and the month of July are extremely lucky for you. The 1st, 8th, 15th and 22nd hours on Mondays will be very powerful. Pay special attention to the new and full Moon days throughout 2009.

The numbers 2, 11 and 29 are lucky for you.

3 = Year of Jupiter

Overview

The year 2009 will be a 3 year for you and, because of this, Jupiter and Sagittarius will dominate your affairs. This is very lucky and shows that you'll be motivated to broaden your horizons, gain more money and become extremely popular in your social circles. It looks like 2009 will be a fun-filled year with much excitement.

Jupiter and Sagittarius are generous to a fault and so likewise, your open-handedness will mark the year. You'll be friendly and helpful to all of those around you.

Pisces is also under the rulership of the number 3 and this brings out your spiritual and compassionate nature. You'll become a much better person, reducing your negative karma by increasing your self-awareness and spiritual feelings. You will want to share your luck with those you love.

Love and pleasure

Travel and seeking new adventures will be part and parcel of your romantic life this year. Travelling to distant lands and meeting unusual people will open your heart to fresh possibilities of romance.

You'll try novel and audacious things and will find yourself in a different circle of friends. Compromise will be important in making your existing relationships work. Talk about your feelings. If you are currently in a relationship you'll feel an upswing in your affection for your partner. This is a perfect opportunity to deepen your love for each other and take your relationship to a new level.

If you're not attached to someone just yet, there's good news for you. Great opportunities lie in store for you and a spiritual or karmic connection may be experienced in 2009.

Work

Great fortune can be expected through your working life in the next twelve months. Your friends and work colleagues will want to help you achieve your goals. Even your employers will be amenable to your requests for extra money or a better position within the organisation.

If you want to start a new job or possibly begin an independent line of business this is a great year to do it. Jupiter looks set to give you plenty of opportunities, success and a superior reputation.

Improving your luck

As long as you can keep a balanced view of things and not overdo anything, your luck will increase dramatically throughout 2009. The important thing is to remain grounded and not be too airy-fairy about your objectives. Be realistic about your talents and capabilities and don't brag about your skills or achievements. This will only invite envy from others.

Moderate your social life as well and don't drink or eat too much as this will slow your reflexes and lessen your chances for success.

You have plenty of spiritual insights this year so you should use them to their maximum. In the 1st, 8th, 15th and 24th hours of Thursdays you should use your intuition to enhance your luck, and the numbers 3, 12, 21 and 30 are also lucky for you. March and December are your lucky months but generally the whole year should go pretty smoothly for you.

4 = Year of Uranus

Overview

The electric and exciting planet of the zodiac Uranus and its sign of Aquarius rule your affairs throughout 2009. Dramatic events will surprise and at the same time unnerve you in your professional and personal life. So be prepared!

You'll be able to achieve many things this year and your dreams are likely to come true, but you mustn't be distracted or scattered with your energies. You'll be breaking through your own self-limitations and this will present challenges from your family and friends. You'll want to be independent and develop your spiritual powers and nothing will stop you.

Try to maintain discipline and an orderly lifestyle so you can make the most of these special energies this year. If unexpected things do happen, it's not a bad idea to have an alternative plan so you don't lose momentum.

Love and pleasure

You want something radical, something different in your relationships this year. It's quite likely that your love life will be feeling a little less than exciting so you'll take some important steps to change that. If your partner is as progressive as you'll be this year, then your relationship is likely to improve and fulfil both of you.

In your social life you will meet some very unusual people whom you'll feel are specially connected to you spiritually. You may want to ditch everything for the excitement and passion of a completely new relationship, but tread carefully as this may not work out exactly as you'd expected.

Work

Technology, computing and the Internet will play a larger role in your professional life this coming year. You'll have to move ahead with the times and learn new skills if you want to achieve success.

A hectic schedule is likely, so make sure your diary is with you at all times. Try to be more efficient and don't waste time.

New friends and alliances at work will help you achieve even greater success in the coming period. Becoming a team player will be even more important towards gaining satisfaction in your professional endeavours.

Improving your luck

Moving too quickly and impulsively will cause you problems on all fronts, so be a little more patient and think your decisions through more carefully. Social, romantic and professional opportunities will come to you but take a little time to investigate the ramifications of your actions.

The 1st, 8th, 15th and 20th hours of any Saturday are lucky, but love and luck are likely to cross your path when you least expect it. The numbers 4, 13, 22 and 31 are also lucky for you this year.

5 = Year of Mercury

Overview

The supreme planet of communication, Mercury, is your ruling planet throughout 2009. The number 5, which is connected to Mercury, will confer upon you success through your intellectual abilities.

Any form of writing or speaking will be improved and this will be, to a large extent, underpinning your success. Your imagination will be stimulated by this planet with many incredible new and exciting ideas coming to mind.

Mercury and the number 5 are considered somewhat indecisive. Be firm in your attitude and don't let too many ideas or opportunities distract and confuse you. By all means get as much information as you can to help you make the right decision.

I see you involved with money proposals, job applications, even contracts that need to be signed so remain clear-headed as much as possible.

Your business skills and clear and concise communication will be at the heart of your life in 2009.

Love and pleasure

Mercury, which rules the signs of Gemini and Virgo, will make your love life a little difficult due to its changeable nature. On the one hand you'll feel passionate and loving to your partner, yet on the other you will feel like giving it all up for the excitement of a new affair. Maintain the middle ground.

Also, try not to be too critical with your friends and family members. The influence of Virgo makes you prone to expecting much more from others than they're capable of giving. Control your sharp tongue and don't hurt people's feelings. Encouraging others is the better path, leading to more emotional satisfaction.

Work

Speed will dominate your professional life in 2009. You'll be flitting from one subject to another and taking on far more than you can handle. You'll need to make some serious changes in your routine to handle the avalanche of work that will come your way. You'll also be travelling with your work, but not necessarily overseas.

If you're in a job you enjoy then this year will give you additional successes. If not, it may be time to move on.

Improving your luck

Communication is the secret of attaining your desires in the coming twelve months. Keep focused on one idea rather than scattering your energies in all directions and your success will be speedier.

By looking after your health, sleeping well and exercising regularly, you'll build up your resilience and mental strength.

The 1st, 8th, 15th and 20th hours of Wednesday are lucky so it's best to schedule your meetings and other important social engagements during these times. The lucky numbers for Mercury are 5, 14, 23 and 32.

6 = Year of Venus

Overview

Because you're ruled by 6 this year, love is in the air! Venus, Taurus and Libra are well known for their affinity with romance, love, and even marriage. If ever you were going to meet a soulmate and feel comfortable in love, 2009 must surely be your year.

Taurus has a strong connection to money and practical affairs as well, so finances will also improve if you are diligent about work and security issues.

The important thing to keep in mind this year is that sharing love and making that important soul connection should be kept high on your agenda. This will be an enjoyable period in your life.

Love and pleasure

Romance is the key thing for you this year and your current relationships will become more fulfilling if you happen to be attached. For singles, a 6 year heralds an important meeting that eventually leads to marriage.

You'll also be interested in fashion, gifts, jewellery and all sorts of socialising. It's at one of these social engagements that you could meet the love of your life. Remain available!

Venus is one of the planets that has a tendency to overdo things, so be moderate in your eating and drinking. Try generally to maintain a modest lifestyle.

Work

You'll have a clearer insight into finances and your future security during a number 6 year. Whereas you may have had additional expenses and extra distractions previously, your mind will be more settled and capable of longer-term planning along these lines.

With the extra cash you might see this year, decorating your home or office will give you a special sort of satisfaction.

Social affairs and professional activities will be strongly linked. Any sort of work-related functions may offer you romantic opportunities as well. On the other hand, be careful not to mix up your workplace relationships with romantic ideals. This could complicate some of your professional activities.

Improving your luck

You'll want more money and a life of leisure and ease in 2009. Keep working on your strengths and eliminate your negative personality traits to create greater luck and harmony in your life.

Moderate all your actions and don't focus exclusively on money and material objects. Feed your spiritual needs as well. By balancing the inner and outer you'll see that your romantic and professional life will be enhanced more easily.

The 1st, 8th, 15th and 20th hours on Fridays will be very lucky for you and new opportunities will arise for you at those times. You can use the numbers 6, 15, 24 and 33 to increase luck in your general affairs.

7 = Year of Neptune

Overview

The last and most evolved sign of the zodiac is Pisces, which is ruled by Neptune. The number 7 is deeply connected with this zodiacal sign and governs you in 2009. Your ideals seem to be clearer and more spiritually orientated than ever before. Your desire to evolve and understand your inner self will be a double-edged sword. It depends on how organised you are as to how well you can use these spiritual and abstract concepts in your practical life.

Your past emotional hurts and deep emotional issues will be dealt with and removed for good, if you are serious about becoming a better human being.

Spend a little more time caring for yourself rather than others, as it's likely some of your friends will drain you of energy with their own personal problems. Of course, you mustn't turn a blind eye to the needs of others, but don't ignore your own personal needs in the process.

Love and pleasure

Meeting people with similar life views and spiritual aspirations will rekindle your faith in relationships. If you do choose to develop a new romance, make sure that there is a clear understanding of the responsibilities of one to the other. Don't get swept off your feet by people who have ulterior motives.

Keep your relationships realistic and see that the most idealistic partnerships must eventually come down to Earth. Deal with the practicalities of life.

Work

This is a year of hard work, but one in which you'll come to understand the deeper significance of your professional ideals. You may discover a whole new aspect to your career, which involves a more compassionate and self-sacrificing side to your personality.

You'll also find that your way of working will change and that you'll be more focused and able to get into the spirit of whatever you do. Finding meaningful work is very likely and therefore this could be a year when money, security, creativity and spirituality overlap to bring you a great sense of personal satisfaction.

Tapping into your greater self through meditation and self-study will bring you great benefits throughout 2009.

Improving your luck

Using self-sacrifice along with discrimination will be an unusual method of improving your luck. The laws of karma state that what you give, you receive in greater measure. This is one of the principal themes for you in 2009.

The 1st, 8th, 15th and 20th hours of Tuesdays are your lucky times. The numbers 7, 16, 25 and 34 should be used to increase your lucky energies.

8 = Year of Saturn

Overview

The earthy and practical sign of Capricorn and its ruler Saturn are intimately linked to the number 8, which rules you in 2009. Your discipline and far-sightedness will help you achieve great things in the coming year. With cautious discernment, slowly but surely you will reach your goals.

It may be that due to the influence of the solitary Saturn, your best work and achievement will be behind closed doors away from the limelight. You mustn't fear this as you'll discover many new things about yourself. You'll learn just how strong you really are.

Love and pleasure

Work will overshadow your personal affairs in 2009, but you mustn't let this erode the personal relationships you have. Becoming a workaholic brings great material successes but will also cause you to become too insular and aloof. Your family members won't take too kindly to you working 100-hour weeks.

Responsibility is one of the key words for this number and you will therefore find yourself in a position of authority that leaves very little time for fun. Try to make time to enjoy the company of friends and family and by all means schedule time off on the weekends as it will give you the peace of mind you're looking for.

Because of your responsible attitude it will be very hard for you not to assume a greater role in your workplace and this indicates longer working hours with the likelihood of a promotion with equally good remuneration.

Work

Money is high on your agenda in 2009. Number 8 is a good money number according to the Chinese and this year is at last likely to bring you the fruits of your hard labour. You are cautious and resourceful in all your dealings and will not waste your hard-earned savings. You will also be very conscious of using your time wisely.

You will be given more responsibilities and you're likely to take them on, if only to prove to yourself that you can handle whatever life dishes up.

Expect a promotion in which you will play a leading role in your work. Your diligence and hard work will pay off, literally, in a bigger salary and more respect from others.

Improving your luck

Caution is one of the key characteristics of the number 8 and is linked to Capricorn. But being overly cautious could cause you to miss valuable opportunities. If an offer is put to you, try to think outside the square and balance it with your naturally cautious nature.

Be gentle and kind to yourself. By loving yourself, others will naturally love you, too. The 1st, 8th, 15th and 20th hours of Saturdays are exceptionally lucky for you as are the numbers 1, 8, 17, 26 and 35.

9 = Year of Mars

Overview

You are now entering the final year of a nine-year cycle dominated by the planet Mars and the sign of Aries. You'll be completing many things and are determined to be successful after several years of intense work.

Some of your relationships may now have reached their use-by date and even these personal affairs may need to be released. Don't let arguments and disagreements get in the road of friendly resolution in these areas of your life.

Mars is a challenging planet and, this year, although you will be very active and productive, you may find others trying to obstruct the achievement of your goals. As a result you may react strongly to them, thereby creating disharmony in your workplace. Don't be so impulsive or reckless, and generally slow things down. The slower, steadier approach has greater merit this year.

Love and pleasure

If you become too bossy and pushy with friends this year you will just end up pushing them out of your life. It's a year to end certain friendships but by the same token it could be the perfect time to end conflicts and thereby bolster your love affairs in 2009.

If you're feeling a little irritable and angry with those you love, try getting rid of these negative feelings through some intense, rigorous sports and physical activity. This will definitely relieve tension and improve your personal life.

Work

Because you're healthy and able to work at a more intense pace you'll achieve an incredible amount in the coming year. Overwork could become a problem if you're not careful.

Because the number 9 and Mars are infused with leadership energy, you'll be asked to take the reins of the job and steer your company or group in a certain direction. This will bring with it added responsibility but also a greater sense of purpose for you.

Improving your luck

Because of the hot and restless energy of the number 9, it is important to create more mental peace in your life this year. Lower the temperature, so to speak, and decompress your relationships rather than becoming aggravated. Try to talk to your work partners and loved ones rather than telling them what to do. This will generally pick up your health and your relationships.

The 1st, 8th, 15th and 20th hours of Tuesdays are the luckiest for you this year and, if you're involved in any disputes or need to attend to health issues, these times are also very good for the best results. Your lucky numbers are 9, 18, 27 and 36.

ARIES

2009:
Your Daily Planner

A failure is a man who has blundered, but is not able to cash in on the experience.

—Elbert Hubbard

There is a little-known branch of astrology called electional astrology, and it can help you select the most appropriate times for many of your day-to-day activities.

Ancient astrologers understood the planetary patterns and how they impacted on each of us. This allowed them to suggest the best possible times to start various important activities. Many farmers today still use this approach: they understand the phases of the Moon, and attest to the fact that planting seeds on certain lunar days produces a far better crop than planting on other days.

The following section covers many areas of daily life, and uses the cycles of the Moon and the combined strength of the other planets to work out the best times to start different types of activity.

So to create your own personal almanac, first select the activity you are interested in, and then quickly scan the year for the best months to start it. When you have selected the month, you can finetune your timing by finding the best specific dates. You can then be sure that the planetary energies will be in sync with you, offering you the best possible outcome.

Coupled with what you know about your monthly and weekly trends, the daily planner can be a powerful tool to help you capitalise on opportunities that come your way this year.

Good luck, and may the planets bless you with great success, fortune and happiness in 2009!

Starting activities

How many times have you made a new year's resolution to begin a diet or be a better person in your relationships? And how many times has it not worked out? Well, the reason may be partly that you started out at the wrong time! How successful you are is strongly influenced by the position of the Moon and the planets when you begin a particular activity. You could be more successful with the following activities if you start them on the days indicated.

Relationships

We all feel more empowered on some days than on others. This is because the planets have some power over us—their movement and their relationships to each other determine the ebb and flow of our energies. And our level of self-confidence and our sense of romantic magnetism play an important part in the way we behave in relationships.

Your daily planner tells you the ideal dates for meeting new friends, initiating a love affair, spending time with family and loved ones—it even tells you the most appropriate times for sexual encounters.

You'll be surprised at how much more impact you make in your relationships when you tune yourself in to the planetary energies on these special dates.

Falling in love/restoring love

During these times you could expect favourable energies to meet your soulmate or, if you've had difficulty in a relationship, to approach the one you love to rekindle both your and their emotional responses:

January	28, 30
February	25, 26
March	6, 7, 8, 28, 29, 30
April	25, 26, 30
May	1, 2, 5, 7, 26, 27, 28, 29

June	2, 3, 23, 24, 26, 29, 30
July	22, 23, 26, 27
August	14, 15, 16, 17, 22, 23, 24
September	10, 14, 16, 19, 20, 21
October	9, 10, 11, 12, 13
November	25, 26
December	22, 23, 27, 31

Special times with friends and family

Socialising, partying and having a good time with those you enjoy being with is highly favourable under the following dates. These dates are excellent to spend time with family and loved ones in a domestic environment:

January	26
February	8, 12, 13, 14, 22, 23, 24
March	8, 22, 23
April	19, 27, 28
May	1, 2, 15, 16, 17, 24, 25, 28, 29
June	2, 3, 11, 12, 13, 22, 30
July	23, 26, 27
August	5, 6, 23, 24
September	16
October	13
November	8, 10, 24
December	19, 20, 21, 29

Healing or resuming relationships

If you're trying to get back together with the one you love and need a heart-to-heart or deep and meaningful, you can try the following dates to do so:

January	5, 8, 11, 12, 18, 19, 20, 21, 22, 23, 24, 25, 26, 28, 30
February	8, 12, 13, 14
March	8
April	18, 19
May	1, 2, 28, 29
June	2, 3, 30
July	23, 26, 27
August	23, 24
September	16
October	13
November	8
December	22, 23, 27

Sexual encounters

Physical and sexual energies are well favoured on the following dates. The energies of the planets enhance your moments of intimacy during these times:

January	5, 30
February	25, 26
March	6, 7, 8, 28, 29, 30
April	25, 26, 30
May	1, 2, 5, 7, 26, 27, 28, 29

June	2, 3, 23, 24, 26, 29, 30
July	22, 23, 26, 27
August	23, 24
September	16
October	13
November	25, 26
December	22, 23, 27, 31

Health and wellbeing

Your aura and life force are susceptible to the movements of the planets; in particular, they respond to the phases of the Moon.

The following dates are the most appropriate times to begin a diet, have cosmetic surgery, or seek medical advice. They also tell you when the best times are to help others.

Feeling of wellbeing

Your physical as well as your mental alertness should be strong on these following dates. You can plan your activities and expect a good response from others:

January	8, 9, 26, 27
February	4, 5, 22, 23
March	31
April	18, 19, 27, 28
May	16, 17
June	21, 22
July	19
August	5, 6, 24, 25

September	12, 28, 30
October	8, 9
November	8, 10
December	19, 20, 21, 29, 30

Healing and medicine

This is good for approaching others who have expertise at a time when you need some deeper understanding. This is also favourable for any sort of healing or medication and making appointments with doctors or psychologists. Planning surgery around these dates should bring good results.

Often giving up our time and energy to assist others doesn't necessarily result in the expected outcome. By lending a helping hand to a friend on the following dates, the results should be favourable:

January	1, 20, 21, 22, 23, 24, 25, 26, 27, 28, 29, 30, 31
February	9, 10, 11, 12, 13, 14, 15, 16, 17, 18, 19, 20, 21, 22, 23, 24, 25, 26, 27, 28
March	2, 3, 4, 5, 6, 7, 8, 9, 22, 26, 28, 29, 30, 31
April	1, 10, 12, 15, 18, 20, 27, 28, 29, 30
May	1, 3, 7, 8, 9, 10, 11, 12
June	6, 7, 9, 13, 14, 15, 19, 21, 22
July	5, 6, 7, 8, 10, 12, 18, 19, 20, 25, 26
August	6, 7, 8, 9, 10, 29, 30, 31
September	1, 6, 27
October	8, 9, 10, 11, 12, 25, 26
November	18, 19, 20, 21, 22
December	10, 11, 12

Money

Money is an important part of life, and involves many decisions; decisions about borrowing, investing, spending. The ideal times for transactions are very much influenced by the planets, and whether your investment or nest egg grows or doesn't grow can often be linked to timing. Making your decisions on the following dates could give you a whole new perspective on your financial future.

Managing wealth and money

To build your nest egg, it's a good time to open your bank account and invest money on the following dates:

January	3, 4, 5, 10, 11, 16, 17, 23, 24, 25, 31
February	1, 6, 7, 12, 13, 14, 20, 21, 27, 28
March	5, 6, 7, 12, 13, 19, 26, 27
April	2, 3, 8, 9, 15, 17, 23, 24, 29, 30
May	5, 6, 7, 13, 14, 20, 21, 26, 27
June	2, 3, 9, 10, 16, 17, 18, 23, 24, 29, 30
July	6, 7, 8, 14, 15, 20, 21, 26, 27
August	2, 3, 4, 10, 11, 17, 18, 23, 24, 30, 31
September	6, 7, 13, 14, 19, 20, 26, 27
October	3, 4, 5, 10, 11, 16, 17, 18, 23, 24, 25, 31
November	1, 6, 7, 13, 14, 20, 21, 27, 28
December	4, 5, 10, 11, 17, 18, 24, 25, 26, 31

Spending

It's always fun to spend but the following dates are more in tune with this activity and are likely to give you better results:

January	20, 28, 30
February	3
March	28, 29, 30
April	25, 26
May	31
June	1, 2, 7, 8, 9, 10, 28, 30
July	1, 2, 3, 26, 27, 29, 30
August	2, 3, 4, 5, 20, 21, 22, 23, 24, 25
September	19, 20, 21, 22, 23
October	9, 10
November	1, 7, 8, 17
December	27, 28

Selling

If you're thinking of selling something, whether it is small or large, consider the following dates as ideal times to do so:

January	3, 18, 19, 20, 21, 25, 26, 27, 28, 29, 30, 31
February	8, 10, 11, 12, 13, 14, 15, 18, 20, 22, 23, 24, 26, 28
March	2, 3, 4, 5, 6, 7, 8, 9, 16, 26, 27, 28, 31
April	5, 10, 19, 20, 23, 25, 27, 28, 29
May	1, 2, 7, 9, 13, 14, 21, 24, 25, 28, 29, 31
June	1, 2, 7, 8, 14, 16, 17, 20, 21, 22, 26, 30
July	1, 2, 3, 9, 10, 11, 15, 16, 17, 26, 27
August	2, 3, 4, 13, 14, 15, 16, 17
September	1, 2, 3, 4, 5, 6, 14, 15, 16, 17, 21, 22, 23, 24, 25, 26, 27, 28, 30, 31

October	1, 2, 3, 4, 5, 6, 7, 8, 9, 10, 11, 12, 31
November	2, 3, 9, 10, 11, 12, 13, 25, 26, 27, 28, 29, 30
December	1, 2, 3, 7, 8, 9, 17, 20

Borrowing

Few of us like to borrow money, but if you must, taking out a loan on the following dates should be positive:

January	11, 18, 19, 20, 23, 24, 25
February	15, 16, 20, 21
March	14, 15, 19, 20
April	10, 11, 12, 15, 16, 17
May	9, 13, 14
June	9, 10
July	7, 8, 20, 21
August	17, 18
September	13, 14
October	10, 11
November	6, 7, 15, 16
December	4, 5, 12, 13, 14

Work and education

Your career is important to you, and continual improvement of your skills is therefore also crucial, professionally, mentally and socially. The dates below will help you find out the most appropriate times to improve your professional talents and commence new work or education associated with your work.

You may need to decide when to start learning a new skill, when to ask for a promotion, and even when to make an important career change. Here are the days when mental and educational power is strong.

Learning new skills

Educational pursuits are lucky and bring good results on the following dates:

January	8, 9
February	4, 5
March	3, 4, 10, 31
April	1, 6, 7, 27, 28
May	3, 4, 25, 30, 31
June	1, 6, 7, 27, 28
July	4, 5, 24, 25, 31
August	1, 21, 22, 27, 28, 29
September	23, 24, 25
October	21, 22
November	17, 18, 19
December	29, 30

Changing career path or profession

If you're feeling stuck and need to move into a new professional activity, changing jobs can be done at these times:

January	6, 7
February	2, 3
March	1, 2, 3, 4, 5, 6, 7, 8, 9, 10, 28, 29, 30
April	6, 7, 25, 26
May	3, 4, 30, 31
June	1, 27, 28

July	6, 24, 25
August	2, 3, 4, 21, 22, 30, 31
September	26, 27
October	23, 24, 25
November	2, 20, 21, 29, 30
December	1, 17, 18, 27, 28

Promotion, professional focus and hard work

To increase your mental focus and achieve good results from the work you do, promotions are likely on these dates that follow:

January	4, 5, 6, 11, 12, 13, 14, 15, 16, 21
February	6
March	18, 19, 20
April	8, 28, 29
May	12, 21
June	25, 26
July	1, 2, 3, 8, 15, 17
August	4, 14, 15, 16, 17, 18, 22, 23, 24
September	14, 15, 18, 19, 23, 24, 25, 26
October	22
November	7, 10, 11, 12, 17
December	1, 2, 3, 7, 28

Travel

Setting out on a holiday or adventurous journey is exciting. To gain the most out of your holidays and journeys, travelling on the following dates is likely to give you a sense of fulfilment:

January	9, 10, 28, 29, 30, 31
February	1, 4, 5, 26
March	3, 4, 5, 6, 7, 27, 31
April	27, 28, 29
May	1, 2, 25
June	6, 7, 25, 26
July	6, 31
August	1, 2, 21, 22, 23, 24, 29
September	19, 20, 23, 24, 25, 26, 27
October	1, 2, 3, 25, 28, 29, 30, 31
November	1, 17, 18, 26, 28
December	17, 18, 23, 26

Beauty and grooming

Believe it or not, cutting your hair or nails has a powerful effect on your body's electromagnetic energy. If you cut your hair or nails at the wrong time of the month, you can reduce your level of vitality significantly. Use these dates to ensure you optimise your energy levels by staying in tune with the stars.

Hair and nails

January	1, 2, 8, 9, 21, 22, 28, 29, 30
February	4, 5, 17, 18, 19, 25, 26
March	3, 4, 16, 17, 18, 24, 25, 31
April	1, 13, 14, 20, 21, 22, 27, 28, 29, 30
May	8, 10, 11, 12, 18, 19, 24, 25
June	6, 7, 8, 14, 15, 21, 22

July	4, 5, 11, 12, 13, 18, 19, 31
August	1, 7, 8, 9, 14, 15, 16, 27, 28, 29
September	4, 5, 11, 12, 23, 24, 25
October	1, 2, 8, 9, 21, 22, 28, 29, 30
November	4, 5, 17, 18, 19, 25, 26
December	2, 3, 15, 16, 22, 23, 29, 30

Therapies, massage and self-pampering

January	18, 19, 20, 26, 27
February	3, 6, 7, 8, 12, 13, 14, 15, 16, 22, 23, 24
March	6, 8, 28, 29, 30
April	5, 8, 9, 18, 19, 25, 26, 29, 30
May	1, 2, 5, 7, 9, 15, 16, 17, 22, 23, 26, 27, 28, 29
June	2, 3, 4, 5, 11, 12, 13, 19, 20, 23, 24, 26, 30
July	1, 2, 3, 9, 10, 23, 26, 27, 28, 29, 30
August	6, 12, 13, 17, 18, 19, 20, 23, 24, 25, 26
September	1, 2, 13, 14, 16
October	10, 11, 12, 13, 16, 17, 27
November	8, 9, 10, 13, 16, 23, 24, 29, 30
December	1, 4, 5, 6, 7, 10, 11, 12, 13, 14, 19, 20, 21, 27, 28, 31

Mills & Boon
100th Birthday Collection
The King's Bride
LUCY GORDON
Mills & Boon
100th Birthday Collection
They're Wed Again
PENNY JORDAN
Mills & Boon
100th Birthday Collection
The Boss's Valentine
LYNNE GRAHAM
ONLY
£1.49!
EACH
Only
£1.49